FAREWELL, OLD GIRL

And Other Stories of the Great Outdoors

~~~~~~

By J. Michael Kelly

FAREWELL, OLD GIRL

And Other Stories of the Great Outdoors

Herald Publishing Co., LLC, Syracuse, N.Y. ©
1991, 1992, 1993, 1994, 1995, 1996, 1997, 1998, 1999,
2000, 2001, 2002, 2003, 2004, 2005, 2006.
The Post-Standard
All rights reserved.
Reprinted with permission.

ISBN: 978-0-9846418-0-2

Library of Congress information:
2011905959

All stories contained in this anthology originally appeared in the Syracuse Post-Standard or Syracuse Herald-American between 1991 and 2006. The author is deeply grateful for the permission granted by one of the nation's finest daily newspapers.

DEDICATION

To Bob, Dan, Tim and other dearly departed friends who can't wait to tell us about the fishing and hunting in the next world – which I believe is even more beautiful than this one.

ACKNOWLEDGEMENTS

It was my great good fortune to spend 36 years as a full-time reporter for The Syracuse Newspapers. The Post-Standard sports editors who processed my "stuff" – Dave Rahme, John Lammers, Steve Carlic and Charlie Miller – were all top-notch professionals who let me be me.

The late Bob Peel – my mentor and immediate predecessor on the outdoors beat at The Post-Standard – greatly influenced my writing style and my conduct as a sportsman. Another since-deceased tutor who helped me to stretch and grow as a writer was Sam Vaccaro, who rode herd on contributors to the paper's Sunday magazine.

I also owe special thanks to my boyhood best friend Dan Skinner, who made me laugh and cry during his valiant but losing battle with leukemia; my Dad, John W. "Chuckle" Kelly, who gave me his love of woods and waters before leaving Mom, my brother and sisters and all the rest of his relatives and friends much too soon; and Mr. Tom Petro, the inspiring 6th-Grade teacher who was the first to suggest I might be able to make a living at this sort of thing.

None of these influences could have forced pen to paper, however. My jump-starters are my children and my wife. Sean and Brenna have always made me proud and Chickie provides an endless reservoir of love and sympathy. How she puts up with me, I'll never know.

TABLE OF CONTENTS

FOREWORD 7

A CREEK RUNS IN THE FAMILY 9

STILL FOR THE BIRDS 13

BIG HEART OVERCOMES BAD BREAK 17

OLD WEST, NEW LOOK 22

IN HEAVEN THERE MUST BE BUGS GALORE 26

DIETERS BEWARE 31

VENISON FEAST IS FIT FOR A KING 35

VETERANS DAY BRINGS MEMORIES OF DAD 38

A HUNTER'S VISION 41

ROCKER KEEPS 'EM REELING 47

IT'S A COYOTE, AND A FEW MORE ANSWERS.... 52

A REWARDING DAY 56

DEER DIARY: YOU'LL NEVER BELIEVE 59

FULFILLMENT FLOWS
FROM NEAREST STREAM 64

THE HUNT: AN ANCIENT INSTINCT 68

CARNIVORES COME IN VARIOUS FORMS 72

WRITER SPEAKS VOLUMES 75

THE BEST PART OF FISHING?
PASSING ON TRADITIONS 77

FAREWELL, OLD GIRL	81
THIS ANGLER ROLLS WITH THE LUNCHES	86
A GRAND FANTASY: IF I WERE KING	89
BROOKIES STILL THE FINEST PRIZE	92
THE ART OF SEDUCTION	96
BIG RAINBOWS AN APRIL CHALLENGE	100
PAPA'S LATEST DESERVES PRAISE	105
HEAVEN CAN WAIT ON THE DELAWARE	108
HOMESPUN ANGLERS	114
JULY OFFERS FISHERMEN SOME NICE DISTRACTIONS	118
THE BEST AND WORST OF TIMES FOR AN ANGLER	120
FRIEND'S SPIRIT FLIES IN FACE OF DEATH	124

FOREWORD

Newspaper and magazine articles by J. Michael Kelly have dominated the writing contests sponsored by the New York State Outdoor Writers Association (NYSOWA) year after year, no matter whom the judges might be. That's no fluke. Kelly's stories do more than tell of his adventures, experiences and acquaintances; they draw you in so that you share the sights, smells, thoughts, feelings and thrills.

"Farewell, Old Girl and Other Stories" is a passport to many such journeys, most of them taking place in Central New York, where the author has lived much of his outdoors life.

In my 40-year career of editing outdoor magazines, ranging from national treasures such as *Field & Stream*, *Outdoor Life* and *Sports Afield* to the more localized gem, *New York Sportsman*, I have had the pleasure of reading the work of some of the most revered outdoor communicators. Mike Kelly's articles share a common thread with those by the literary greats: they make their words yours. You embrace each story, and relate to its message. These are gifts to readers. You hold in your hand such a present. Savor its contents.

Glenn Sapir, President
NYSOWA

Soon after marrying into the Kelly family, Bill McPartland of Baldwinsville got the hang of fishing in Nine Mile Creek.

A CREEK RUNS IN THE FAMILY
June 4, 1996

Rain, floods and erosion transformed my old friend into a sullen stranger this spring, but I take comfort in knowing Nine Mile Creek has endured much worse punishment over the years.

The creek flowed in patriotic reds, whites and blues during World War II, as leftover dyes were flushed into its pools by local woolen mills.

In the early 1960s, thousands of brown and brook trout went belly-up, reportedly after tree sprayers rinsed a pesticide tanker on the stream banks.

Then, just as Nine Mile was recovering from that devastating fish kill, road builders yanked some of its prettiest bends straight as a flagpole so commuters could zip between Camillus and Marcellus a few minutes faster.

Fishermen who marvel at the beauty of the creek today should have seen it when the Beatles had short hair and the Empire State Building was still the tallest in the world.

In those days Nine Mile glided under stonework bridges, past sturdy brick mills that made enough bolt cloth and wrapping paper to support double shifts of workers.

Below Marcellus Falls, the stream divided into two channels that went their separate ways for about a quarter-mile before mingling again.

When I was in junior high school a new teacher asked a classmate where he lived. She sent Charlie to the principal's office for smartly responding that he resided on an island in Nine Mile Creek, but he was telling the truth. His house was on Route 174, between the bridges that spanned the east and west branches of the stream.

One summer my father noticed that Charlie's parents sometimes tossed their kitchen scraps into the creek. He turned their bad habit to his advantage by using a kernel of canned corn to catch a 13-inch brook trout, its stomach bulging with mixed vegetables.

The bridge at the head of the island shaded a deep bend pool the locals knew as Gleason's after the owner of the tavern that stood a few yards up the road.

During the Great Depression, my grandfather Kelly saw a torpedo shape in Gleason's tucked beneath the bridge supports. He fished for weeks with worms, minnows and other traditional baits but couldn't seduce the lunker.

Finally, Grandpa live-trapped a mouse in the paper mill where he worked. He slipped a rubber band around the wriggling creature and then poked a size 2 hook under the makeshift girdle.

A whirlpool engulfed the rodent when it drifted under the bridge. The hook-jawed brown that flopped on the grass a few minutes later was 27 inches long. Decades afterward, Marcellus fishermen recalled Grandpa's trophy as the biggest trout ever caught in Nine Mile.

Engineers obliterated that pool and many others when the road was rebuilt. The creek branch behind Charlie's house was diverted into the other channel, and the springs that seeped from limestone cliffs to sustain its brook trout through the hottest summers now trickle onto dry ground.

The boulder-strewn runs below the island were smoothed into a single, 200-yard riffle. Gently sloping banks and towering shade trees made way for gabion walls and transplanted saplings.

It was heartbreaking to see the creek channeled, but its trout adjusted surprisingly well to the new contours. The long flat below the improved highway became one of the best dry-fly pools in the stream.

As polluting mills went broke and state and federal grants paid for municipal sewer improvements, Nine Mine put on a shiny new face, but someone or something has always been available to scuff it up a bit.

The creek is lined with black willows that inevitably are toppled by gales or their own massive weight. One of the giant trees crushed the throat of my father's favorite pool in the swamp north of the Martisco Railroad about a dozen years ago. Dad gave it a few casts every spring until the year he died, but the spot was never the same.

My own pet pool, formed by the digging of swift currents at the base of a bridge abutment, was ruined by state highway crews. It was neck-deep one day but barely covered my ankles the next. Standing in the bulldozer's tracks, I thought of the 22-inch brown that lived in that pool many years before. When it stripped line after inhaling my nightcrawler one drizzly August morning, I assumed the fish was a carp, because I could not imagine a trout so large and strong. I was about to break it off in disgust when my cousin Matt peered into the water and saw black and red spots.

Today, I would release such a trout in the hope it might

father more like itself, but few 13-year-olds are so far-sighted. I skulled my prize with a rock, lugged it to the road and proudly held it aloft for passing motorists to admire.

Several other four-pounders occupied the same pool in the seasons that followed, and I had a passing acquaintance with most of them.

Now, the lunker hole was gone forever, and my youth with it. I could not bear to fish the bridge stretch for the next two seasons.

But last June I noticed trout rising just below the span, during an evening mayfly hatch. Several took my spent-wing imitations just before dark.

Perhaps the winter floods were not entirely the devil's handiwork, for the churning currents made a good beginning on a new pool at the downstream end of the bridge.

Though lacking the gloomy nooks and crannies that distinguished its predecessor, it is thigh-deep and well-shaded. With time and more high water, it might turn out to be pretty special.

STILL FOR THE BIRDS
November 5, 2004

At age 87, hunter Evan Crim of Radisson has pursued a variety of big-and small-game animals in a lot of places – Wyoming, Scotland and the Yukon among them – but some of his most rewarding days were spent chasing ring-necked pheasants, right here in Onondaga County.

Crim and his hunting buddies, 82-year-old Milt Trach of Galeville and 81-year-old Bob Himpler of Solvay, are familiar faces to anyone who regularly visits the Three Rivers Wildlife Management Area during the autumn months.

From mid-October through mid-December, the veteran sportsmen haunt the public hunting ground just north of Baldwinsville More weekdays than not, one, two or all three of them can be found tramping the WMA fields, shotguns at the ready for flushing birds.

"We don't get around like we used to," admitted Crim. "But we still have a lot of fun."

With nearly two centuries of hunting experiences among them, the trio still have what it takes to bag a ringneck. In fact, one day last fall they each shot the legal limit of two cockbirds per hunter.

Before and after their outings, the friends enjoy kibitzing with other hunters in the Three Rivers parking area on Hencle Boulevard, just east of the railroad tracks.

Crim owned a furniture store in Central Square until

his retirement in 1984, then moved to Radisson with his wife, Norma, now 83. Between hunting seasons, the couple still plays golf three or four times a week.

Trach, who has lived in the same house since he was three months old, operated a dairy farm north of Constantia and also spent 25 years working at Camden Wire.

Himpler, one of 11 children, had a 40-year career as a carpenter.

"I'd hunted partridge (ruffed grouse) and woodcock with Milt for a long time," Crim said. "We met Bob over here at the management area about 20 years ago and have been hunting with him ever since."

"We used to hunt all over," Himpler said. "Not just Three Rivers."

Before the northern part of Onondaga County became heavily developed, he said, some of his favorite ringneck spots were in Cicero and Clay.

"There were birds everywhere," he said.

Trach is the most experienced pheasant hunter of the group. In one 13-year period, he and a nephew and their two Brittanies teamed up to kill 600 ringnecks, an average of approximately 50 each season.

"I started hunting pheasants on the farm when I was a kid," he said. "And I've been hunting them at Three Rivers since 1956. But I had to talk Evan into trying it."

Crim, who has hunted Dall sheep in Alaska, elk in Wyoming and red grouse in Scotland, at first felt pheasants wouldn't be much of a challenge.

"He thought they were too slow," said Trach, with a smile. "He found out different, though."

The three hunters shake their heads when they hear someone speak disdainfully of the pen-reared pheasants that the state Department of Environmental Conservation stocks at public hunting areas in Central New York.

"That's bull," Himpler said. "They're stocked birds, yes. But you still have to hunt them, and they're still fun."

The best way to be successful at the WMA, the three hunters advise, is to hunt it soon after stocking, when birds are most abundant. Timing it right is a matter of luck and persistence, since DEC workers don't announce stocking dates in advance, but release Three Rivers' annual allocation of about 700 pheasants in seven or eight batches during the course of the hunting season.

"We just come and hope they stock that day," said Trach. "And if they don't do it one day, we just figure the odds are that much better they'll stock the following day."

Between stocking truck visits, Crim recommends hunting the thick hedgerows and woods areas of Three Rivers. That's where surviving birds take cover once they've been shot at," he said.

"You might pick up an occasional partridge, too, especially in the woods back in from Sixty Road," Crim added.

As the years pass, the three hunters find that bagging pheasants seems less important than sharing each other's company and watching a good bird dog work a field.

Ah, those dogs. What upland hunter doesn't mist up, remembering the prowess and personality of a beloved canine?

Among them, Crim, Trach and Himpler have owned 17

Brittanies. Himpler's 11-month-old pup, Jake, is his eighth. Last year he said goodbye to Molly, who just might have been his favorite, after a dozen hunting seasons.

Crim smiles when he thinks about a stunt his old Brit Penny used to pull.

"She'd retrieve a bird you shot, drop it at your feet, then point it all over again," he said.

Pete, Trach's plucky companion until 1999, loved hunting almost as much as his master did.

"He lived to be 13 ½," said Trach. "He hunted right through that last season and died two days after it ended."

BIG HEART OVERCOMES BAD BREAK
November 24, 1996

The cock pheasant erupted from the tall grass at the Three Rivers Wildlife Management Area, leveled off 10 feet above the ground and sailed straight over me. I let it pass, then swung through and slapped the trigger.

The bird spun end over end. Uh-oh.

"Harley, get it," I hissed.

But my English springer spaniel was already hot on the trail of the wing-shot bird. She plunged into the weedy patch where the rooster had gone down, made a sharp right-angle turn, then sprinted into a waterlogged wood lot.

A minute later, I heard a throttled "cawk."

Harley stood atop the bird like Tarzan triumphant, feathers hanging from her mouth.

"Good girl," I said. "That's a good girl."

I hope you'll forgive me for bragging a little about my dog, because a year ago it looked as if her hunting days were over.

That November evening I let her outdoors for her daily constitutional and made a couple of phone calls. Twenty minutes later, my wife, Chickie, and I were startled by a knocking at the kitchen door.

A small boy stood on the porch.

"Do you own a black and white dog?" he asked.

"Yes, we do," I said, not realizing Harley was still out. "Why?"

"She's been hit by a car," the boy said.

Throwing on our coats, we ran 100 yards down the street, where shadowy figures were illuminated by a van's flashing emergency lights.

A voice in the crowd – I can't recall a single face – said a car had clipped my dog and kept on going. When the next driver pulled over to assist her, Harley crawled under the vehicle and would not come out.

She barked and snarled and wriggled deeper into her hiding place when I reached for her collar.

The dog that greeted me joyously each day after work and paraded with a favorite toy in her mouth until I knelt to rub her belly did not even recognize me.

After several scary near-misses, I finally managed to cover her with a blanket and slid her from beneath the van.

The trip to the DeWitt Animal Hospital's emergency room was full of self-recrimination. How could I have left Harley outdoors unattended?

En route, I found myself drifting back to another drive, three years earlier, when my wife took the wheel while I held a fat, squirming puppy against my chest. We named her after a spunky female soap opera character – the since-departed Harley Davidson Cooper of "The Guiding Light."

That fall, Harley flushed her first pheasant, at the age of 6 months, and by the following season became a menace to every ringneck within sniffing distance. She was not only a devoted companion but the best bird dog I had ever owned.

What if she died?

At the clinic, X-rays revealed a sharp sliver of bone protruding from Harley's pelvis at a 45-degree angle. Her right hip socket was shattered like a dropped egg. Fortunately, her spinal column was intact and there was no evidence of brain damage.

After watching her overnight, the emergency staff released Harley to our care and recommended we consult with surgeons at the Camillus Animal Clinic.

Doctors David Beyel and Jack Fine, partners at the Camillus facility, recommended we give Harley's bones a few weeks to heal before making a final decision on surgery.

They showed us how to support her with a rolled-towel sling, wheelbarrow fashion, whenever she needed to go outside. She wet on the rug once, her first day home, but did her duty in the yard thereafter, hobbling with our help.

At night, we took turns sleeping on the living-room floor to make sure she kept still.

After six weeks, Harley was strong enough to do without the sling and walked with only a slight limp. But when Dr. Fine rotated her right leg, it made a nut-cracking sound in the socket. Without surgery, painful arthritis would inevitably develop in Harley's hip, he said. He recommended femoral head-and-neck surgery. Beyel, who had performed the operation many times, would saw off the rounded top end of Harley's thigh bone at an angle. She would be left with a sort of false joint, supported by bulked-up leg muscles.

I was almost ashamed to ask, except I knew it would mean as much to Harley as it did to me.

"Will she be able to hunt?" I wondered.

The dog would function normally, although she might continue to limp somewhat, Fine predicted. He knew of a Labrador retriever pup that enjoyed nine active years after undergoing the surgery on both rear legs.

Three days later, Harley was back in her towel sling. A foot-long row of stitches marked the path of the surgeon's knife.

The dog's subsequent recovery was inspiring. By May, she romped after backyard squirrels – although never again out of my sight – and in July Harley took a strength-building swim in Nine Mile Creek.

After Labor Day, I began running her in local fields and could tell immediately she had lost none of her desire to hunt. I splurged on a membership at an area shooting preserve to give her as much field work as possible. It has been rewarding to see her steady progress and the admiration in the eyes of my hunting buddies.

Now, don't get the idea that Harley is perfect. She has been known to raid the garbage can under the sink now and then, and some of our dinner guests have honed her natural begging instincts by tossing tidbits from the table when we weren't looking.

And, although she will fetch a feathered dummy time after time in our yard, she has so far refused to bring a dead pheasant to hand.

I can put up with these shortcomings. As far as I'm

concerned, a little gumption goes a long way, and Harley's heart practically fills her chest.

OLD WEST, NEW LOOK
August 19, 1999

No gambler would give a plugged nickel for his chances, but "Snake Oil" Rob Sigond knew he couldn't back down. He'd brought his herd of longhorns to far to lose it now.

The cowboy from Ballston Spa dropped his plate of beans and grabbed for his gun.

As the Colt barked, rustlers spilled from their saddles, one by one. When his revolver was empty, Snake Oil drew its mate from his other holster, and spat out another hailstorm of lead. As the last of the owlhoots high-tailed it over the ridge, he lever-actioned a final volley with his Winchester Model 73.

Seconds after it started, the gunfight was over.

"Nice shooting, Snake Oil," drawled Sigond's sidekick, "Colorado Ralph" Meyer of Oneida.

Or was that "Kid Trigger?" Naw, maybe it was "Arizona." Shucks, pardner, it's hard to keep track of which cowboy says what, when so many are corralled in one place.

Thirty hombres holed up at the Chittenango Rod & Gun Club Saturday, for the monthly rendezvous of the Bar-20, Inc. Cowboy Action Shooting Club.

They were a bunch of deadeyes, and fancy dressers, to boot.

Cowboy Action Shooting, born just 20 years ago, is one of the fastest-growing shooting sports in the world, with more than 29,000 dues-paying members in its governing body, the Single Action Shooting Society (SASS).

Participants in SASS events take western aliases and don 10-gallon hats and silver spurs for their matches. Under the watchful eye of "trail boss" safety officers, they pepper foot-square steel targets with bullets shot from Old West firearms, such as the Colt .45 Peacemaker and the Smith & Wesson Frontier.

While trap shooters or marksmen in modern rifle matches vie in "rounds" or "flights," Cowboy Action contestants compete, one at a time, in "scenarios" which are based on historic events, John Wayne movies or pure fantasy.

Besides the showdown with the rustlers, Saturday's scenarios included a thrilling train robbery. Competitors bested the bad guys with an elaborate wooden locomotive as a backdrop. It was built by three Bar-20 members, and hauled to the rod and gun club on a flatbed truck.

If you're starting to feel a little nostalgic for your days of yesteryear, you understand what makes these range riders tick.

"We all grew up watching Roy Rogers and Hopalong Cassidy on TV," said Cleveland resident Wayne "Colt Younger" Cripe, the president of the Bar-20. "We were all B-western fans."

Cripe credits Bob "Lone Rider" Crossman of West Winfield with bringing the Cowboy Action craze to New York.

"He was the first SASS member around here," Cripe said. "He and about six others started shooting at his place in 1992."

A year later, Claude "Buck Peters" Gosney of Morrisville and a handful of others formed the Bar-20 and began holding regular shoots at the Chittenango club grounds, which are on Gee Road in the Madison County town of Sullivan. The 40-member club is now one of eight SASS affiliates in the Empire State.

Cripe, who had previously been a competitive handgun shooter, said he saw one scenario in 1994 and "that was all it took" for him to become member 4,488 of SASS.

Although somebody always keeps score of hits, missed and firing times when the Bar-20 convenes, few of the shootists care who wins or loses. The emphasis is on safety and fun, in that order.

"If you're top gun for the day, all you win is bragging rights," said Cripe. "There's no money to win, no prizes."

Some shiny trophies are up for grabs at End of Trail, the annual World Championship of Cowboy Action Shooting held each April in Norco, Calif. But that event is low-key, too. Many of the 500 or more dudes and belles n attendance covet the "best costume" prize more than marksman honors.

Smile when you talk about a SASS member's duds, stranger. End of Trail and statewide roundups such as Georgia's "Mule Camp" and Indiana's "Big Rock" attract throngs of outlaws, marshals, riverboat gamblers and saloon singers – none of whom have a Stetson or sleeve garter out of place. Clothes that don't conform to the fashion standards of the post-Civil War, pre-1900 west just don't cut it with this crowd, and can even be grounds for disqualification.

Baseball caps, short-sleeved shirts and such won't get you past the hitching post at the Bar-20, either.

"Spectators are always welcome, and a rookie shooter doesn't have to be perfectly dressed, but you'd best be prepared the second time you come," Cripe said.

One member of the Bar-20 gang who stands tall in the saddle, outfit-wise, is George Smith of Moravia, better known to his fellow posse members as "Six-Gun Smitty."

The retired construction electrician ordered his wide-brimmed hat and jangly spurs from a cowboy catalog, but he found his breeches and shirt at a Salvation Army thrift store, and made his own leather holsters.

Smith is especially proud of his shooting irons, which have his nickname and his SASS membership number – 369 – engraved on their backplates.

"They're real Colt .45s, not Italian-made copies," he said.

Both guns were built as collector items, one to commemorate the company's 125th anniversary, the other to mark the building of the Alaska pipeline.

"Lots of people have told me they're too valuable to actually shoot, but I want to use them, not look at them," Smith said. "Their next owner can hang them on a wall if he likes."

IN HEAVEN THERE MUST BE BUGS GALORE
June 1, 1997

If heaven is all it's cracked up to be, it must have one heck of a sulfur hatch.

The sulfurs are the creamy butter-colored mayflies that emerge by the millions from Central New York trout streams each May and June. Any fly fisher who happens to be on the water during this annual bug blizzard is bound to conclude that he has one wader-clad foot in paradise.

Trout go crazy when the sulfurs are on.

The mayflies are a mere 6 to 9 millimeters long, but they hatch in such profusion that even the tubbiest brown or rainbow can stuff its stomach with them, one winged tidbit at a time.

Like other mayflies, sulfurs spend most of their lives crawling about stream bottoms. They swim to the surface, sprout wings and fly into riverside treetops when it's time to mate. A day or two after emerging from the water, male and female sulfurs gather in huge, swirling swarms over riffles. They couple in midair – quite an acrobatic feat – and then fall to the water to lay their eggs and die. Hungry trout nail them coming and going.

This year's sulfur hatch may go down in angling diaries as one of the best ever. The seasonal symphony began with a few soft notes about 10 days ago and quickly built to a lasting crescendo. It will last another month, at least.

Syracuse-area sulfurs are actually three insects, but two of the trio, *Ephemerella invaria* and *Ephemerella rotunda*, are such look-alikes that neither trout nor angler can tell them apart without a magnifying glass.

The third species, *Ephemerella dorothea*, is smaller and a brighter yellow than the others and doesn't make its first appearance on the stage until its cousins are heading for the exits.

Invaria and *rotunda* are sometimes referred to as "light Hendricksons." They start popping through the surface any time from 5 p.m. to sunset but tend to emerge later in the day as the hatch continues and the weather warms.

Dorothea, which typically appear from about June 5 until June 30 or so in this region, are known as "pale evening duns" because they wait until nearly dusk to hatch.

Our best local streams, including Nine Mile, Skaneateles, Butternut, Limestone and Chittenango creeks, have rich populations of sulfurs, and any fly fisher who doesn't schedule a couple of evenings on such waters this time of year might as well take up golf.

The other day I arrived at a favorite stretch of Nine Mile at about 6 p.m., just as a *rotunda* or *invaria* lifted off the water with a small brown trout in vain, leaping pursuit. Since it was too early in the evening for a full-blown hatch, I knotted a dark brown imitation mayfly nymph to my leader. I pinched on a BB-size split shot about 18 inches above the hook and began drifting the rig through a series of pools, all the while watching for emerging flies and rising trout.

Several nice browns nabbed the nymph in the next hour and a half, but as shadows crept down the western slope of the Martisco valley, the pock marks of feeding fish began to dent the smooth surface with exciting frequency. I tied on a dry fly pattern and walked upstream to a long pool with a riffle at its head.

Squadrons of swallows were skimming the surface in anticipation of a feast. They picked off climbing mayflies, each in turn, until suddenly there were many more bugs than birds. At first the rises were sporadic, a trout here, a trout there. Then one fish began to feed steadily in the tail of the pool, and another gorged at its head. At 8:15 p.m., a dozen trout were slashing and splashing in rapid sequence.

Mayfly hatches are often brief affairs, and calorie-craving trout are inclined to take whatever stage of insect happens to be most readily available at any given moment.

When a sulfur hatch begins, the emergent nymphs wriggling toward the surface are easy pickings. Then fish are apt to target the duns, or newly winged mayflies, which usually drift only a few inches before flying off. Finally, just before dark, trout key on the spent, egg-laying mayflies, called "spinners," which float helplessly downstream.

Or so all the fishing books say.

On this evening, some fish gulped duns from the surface, while others stuck to nymphs. I had to change flies repeatedly to keep up with the finicky moods of individual trout.

By 8:45, however, there was no doubt about the menu. A soggy parade of spinners glided by in the failing light. The splashy sounds made by trout in desperate pursuit of emerging nymphs and duns was replaced by soft, leisurely gulps.

Bruce Douglas of Syracuse is surrounded during a post-sunset mayfly hatch on West Canada Creek.

I plucked a spinner imitation, with rusty fur body and glossy antron yarn wings, from my vest and was quickly into a 12-incher.

Trout were dimpling all around me as I let that one go, but the curtain was about to fall on my fun.

As I lifted the fly from the water after a fruitless cast, something went bump in the night.

It was a brown bat, banging against the rod tip. He and a dozen of his leather-winged colleagues were flapping around the pool. When I felt the breeze of beating wings on my nose, I knew it was time to reel up and grope my way back to the car.

I'm not really afraid of bats, but the thought of hooking one on a back cast makes me shudder. A friend caught a bat once, on a size 14 Badger Bivisible dry fly. It put up an amazing fight, too, weaving a double-tapered fly line back and forth through a grove of alders.

It was pitch-dark when I finally turned out of the parking area and drove south along the creek, but one angler who had planted himself in the pool upstream from mine wasn't ready to quit.

From the road, I could just make out the glow of his flashlight as he rummaged through fly boxes, in search of a pattern that would take one last trout.

DIETERS BEWARE
May 29, 2003

If you're on a diet, turn the page quick, before it's too late.

A Thousand Islands shore dinner is no place for calorie-counters, to say nothing of the faint of heart. It is, however, an epicurean experience that every St. Lawrence River angler should savor at least once – after consulting with a physician.

"This kind of food is why every fishing guide I know of around here died of a heart attack," said Al Benas, the guide who runs the Thousand Islands Inn in Clayton. "I haven't had a heart attack but I did have a bypass operation."

St. Lawrence guides have been adhering to the same basic shore lunch menu since the 1880s. The feast starts with sizzling fatback and ends with gulps of hot, black coffee. In between springs forth a gourmand's dream and a cardiologist's nightmare.

A dozen members of the sporting press savored not one, but two, such repasts a couple of weekends ago, during the New York State Outdoor Writers Association's annual Spring Safari.

The hook-and-bullet scribes gathered in Clayton to fish, hunt, catch up on professional gossip and break bread.

Benas and fellow guide Myrle Bauer of Clayton don't fool around where that bread is concerned. Every slice served by Benas during a midday Grindstone Island fishing break and Bauer at an evening cook-out in the Thousand Islands Antique Boat Museum pavilion was either deep-fried or filled with something deep-fried.

Old-time Thousand Island guides don't have "poached" or "fat-free" in their vocabulary. A shore lunch simply wouldn't be the same if the chef took a healthy approach to food preparation.

Benas has served hundreds of shore meals since he began guiding bass, pike and muskie fishermen in 1978. Every one of them began with a crackling wood fire and the rendering of a chopped-up hunk of pork fatback in a cast-iron frying pan.

"You can use lard," Benas said. "But it's not authentic."

The salivating commences when the fatback has been heated to a rapid boil and all the diners have wrapped their hands around cold drinks.

Golden brown chips of pork are plucked from the pan and heaped with slices of raw onions on white bread. The fragrant sandwiches serve as salty appetizers for the ensuing feast.

Next comes a big bowl of lettuce, tomatoes, cucumbers and onions. Just one condiment will do for the salad. That's a Thousand Island dressing, preferably the original recipe that was first served to the public more than 100 years ago at the hotel and restaurant Benas now owns.

While the salad is being consumed, salt potatoes boil in large kettle. Between the pot's double lids, ears of sweet corn begin to steam.

The main course is the catch of the day, dipped in flour

or cracker crumbs and fried in pork fat. Fresh northern pike, succulent yellow perch or plump smallmouth bass are the typical fare, but in a pinch modern guides will bail out luckless clients with frozen fillets or – as a last resort – a heap of chicken fingers.

Is there room for dessert? Silly question.

The *piece de resistance* of an island feast is French toast, fried in that same fatback, topped with indelicate dollops of cream, maple syrup and brandy and washed down with steaming campfire coffee.

"That's some of the best coffee you ever drank," Benas assured his writer-guests, and it was.

Not long ago, shore dinners seemed about to fade into the mists of history. Cooking spots were scarce, due to heavy posting and rising real estate prices in the Thousand Islands.

Then, two years ago, the New York State Parks Commission struck a blow for tradition by setting aside part of Grindstone Island for fishing guides with a culinary bent.

Members of the Clayton Guides Association cemented the deal by constructing a new block fireplace, placing four picnic tables and repairing the existing dock, which borders on Eel Bay. Last summer, the Picnic Point site was used regularly.

Central New Yorkers who would like to experience a vintage shore lunch for themselves can do so by booking a day of fishing with Benas at (315) 686-3030 or Bauer at (315) 686-2122.

Their fellow members of the Clayton Guides Association,

who can be contacted at (800) 252-9806, also are on familiar terms with fatback.

VENISON FEAST IS FIT FOR A KING
February 18, 1999

Sorry, but I just can't relate to vegetarians. Every time a tender, juicy morsel of venison slips past my gums I offer silent thanks that I inherited a good set of teeth and a hearty appetite for red meat.

The other night I was in a state of carnivorous rapture. A portion of Venison Wellington flashed across my plate. The steaming steak resting on a bed of mushrooms and shallots and wrapped in a flaky blanket of puff pastry was food fit for a king, but it belonged to me, the crassest of commoners.

My mouth waters at the memory of it.

Anyone who dismisses venison as having a "gamey" flavor is either the victim of a poor cook or possessed of much more discriminating taste buds than mine.

I suspect most unkind opinions of deer meat can be traced to overcooking. Because venison is extremely lean, containing only 153 calories and 1.4 grams of fat per 3.5-ounce serving, it can be rendered dry and chewy in a hurry. To eliminate that possibility, venison should be broiled or fried to no more than medium doneness or prepared with slow, moist-cooking methods.

My kitchen shelf is stocked with a dozen game cookbooks containing hundreds of venison recipes, and I have found very few that don't produce satisfying results.

However, the Venison Wellington was a particular triumph.

If you'd like to judge for yourself, take four small loin or round steaks and remove all traces of bone, tallow and silver-skin. Moisten a large non-stick frying pan with vegetable cooking spray, then cook the steaks over medium heat for about four or five minutes, turning once. Put them in a shallow dish and sprinkle lightly with black pepper and two tablespoons of brandy.

Next, put the meat aside and set your baking oven at 425 degrees.

In the frying pan, cook three cups of fresh, chopped mushrooms and a half cup of finely chopped shallots in a tablespoon of butter or margarine for eight to 10 minute on medium heat. Meanwhile, separate an egg into two bowls. Slightly beat the white and whisk the yolk portion with two tablespoons of skim milk.

Coat a baking sheet with the non-stick vegetable spray. Take a sheet of thawed frozen puff pastry – half of a 17-ounce package – and cut it into four six-inch squares. Spoon about a fourth of the mushrooms and shallots into the center of each square, then top with the steaks. Brush the edge of each pastry square with egg white, then bring the corners of the squares up and over the steaks. Pinch them together, brush with the beaten yolks and put the completed packets on the baking sheet.

Bake the meat-stuffed pastries for 10 minutes, then turn the heat down to 350 degrees and bake another six to 10 minutes, until golden brown.

Another fancy presentation you might want to try on guests who are skeptical of venison is Steak Oscar. Broil tenderloins or loin chops to medium-rare, then remove from the heat long enough to top with chunks of crabmeat and tender-crisp asparagus before finishing to the desired state of doneness. Top with béarnaise sauce.

In truth, though, the simplest of venison dishes are among the most succulent. Spaghetti with venison meatballs is a staple at our house, and nothing tastes better on a cold Saturday night than a venison burger topped with a dollop of catsup and, if you like, a slice of sweet onion.

Some butchers add a bit of beef suet or ground pork to their ground venison, but I would rather have mine straight up. It is healthier that way and exactly as nature intended.

VETERANS DAY BEARS MEMORIES OF DAD
November 14, 2000

Americans used to mark Veterans Day by gathering at war monuments and listening respectfully as politicians or decorated war heroes gave somber speeches at "the eleventh hour of the eleventh day of the eleventh month."

In these times, there are few formal tributes on Nov. 11, but the majority of us mark the date by remembering, in our own way, friends and relatives who defended the nation in its hour of need.

I spent part of the recent holiday hunting ring-necked pheasants, and not coincidentally thinking about my dad, a World War II veteran who died of cancer nine years ago. John W. "Chuckle" Kelly loved few things better than rousting ring-necks in the company of a lively springer spaniel, and if he were still with us he might have been tramping the fields on Thursday, himself.

Dad's obituary made only passing reference to his military service, noting that he jointed the Army immediately after graduating from Marcellus Central High School and served in Europe. The story had much more to say about his passion for the outdoors and his devotion to his family. It noted that he "knew every inch of Nine Mile Creek" and taught each of his seven kids how to fish for trout. I thought the article perfectly captured my father's essential goodness and strong character.

Like most soldiers of his generation, Dad talked very little about the war, although he spoke often of the good times he and his brothers and their friends shared in the years following the conflict.

Growing up, I was aware that Dad had fought against the Germans and that he was a private first class in Patton's 3rd Army. He occasionally allowed me to rummage through his shoe box of war souvenirs, and once even handed me a bound history of Patton's outfit. Unfortunately, the magazine-size report was so dryly written that I never managed to digest more than a few pages of it.

Whenever his young son would ask him what war was like, Dad either told a couple of funny stories about his old comrades in arms or began talking about a totally unrelated subject.

A few years before he died, on a Saturday afternoon when both of us had drunk too many beers and a war movie was on the local tavern's TV screen, Dad surprised me by recounting the time his outfit liberated a Nazi concentration camp. I don't remember which camp it was, but I will never forget what my father said about it.

"I couldn't believe anyone could do that to another human being," he said. Briefly, I saw a mist in his eyes.

And then, just like that, he changed the subject.

Although I was barely acquainted with my father the soldier, I know well the boy he was when the trumpets of war summoned him.

Dad loved hunting, fishing, baseball, matinee double features and the innocence of small-town life. Like all the men and women we honor on Veterans Day, he bravely put such things aside, simply because his country asked him to.

The author's father and his springer spaniel, Perky, on a 1970s pheasant hunt.

A HUNTER'S VISION
September 15, 1996

Perched in her tree stand, Canandaigua bowhunter Sharon Pagel could hear a large animal picking its way along the brush-covered hill.

"It's a doe," her husband, Tom, whispered in her ear.

The deer passed within 10 feet of the tree. Sharon thought about shooting, but decided to hold her aim, in case a buck followed the doe down the trail.

"And that's just what happened," she recalled. "A few minutes later, here comes this little spikehorn."

When the buck stopped broadside, 12 yards away, Pagel drew her bow. Tim gently adjusted here aim by twisting her left forearm, and breathed the word "now."

"It was remarkable," Sharon said. "I felt so calm, doing exactly what Tim told me to do. I heard the arrow release and the snap of the bow string. I could even hear the arrow strike the deer."

The deer bucked, ran less than 100 yards and fell to the ground.

"You got him," Tim told Sharon.

She was so excited she threw her arms around Tim's neck.

"I practically strangled him, I hugged him so hard," she said.

That November 1995 buck was Sharon's first with a

bow — and the first deer she had taken since she became blind.

Pagel, 51, is a dedicated hunter who has killed dozens of whitetails over the years with her shotgun. But in late 1994 she thought her treasured times in the woods had come to an end.

"I checked into Strong Memorial Hospital (in Rochester) for what was supposed to be a pretty routine lower back operation," she said. "But when I woke up afterward, I couldn't see."

Her optic nerve was damaged during the surgery. The doctors told her the vision loss was permanent.

"At that moment, my whole world fell apart," she said. "My first coherent thought was, 'My God, I'm never going to be able to hunt again.'"

Tim and Sharon Pagel had shot and hunted together for most of their 18 years of marriage. They taught state hunter-education classes and instructed neophyte archers at the Boy Scouts' Camp Cutler and at a Canandaigua gun shop.

"I worked at home, as a taxidermist, and I got so I would just pick up my bow and go hunting for an hour or two whenever I felt like it," she recalled. "It didn't even matter if I got a deer; it was just great being out there."

Between bow seasons, Tim and Sharon and their son Jeff spent many happy hours shooting at the local archery range.

"We shot for ice cream," she said. "Loser buys."

She couldn't imagine giving that up, and, fortunately, neither could her husband.

After talking with archers who had triumphed over paralysis, amputated limbs and other impairments with the help of customized bows, Tim set out to build a new bow sight that would let Sharon take aim through his eyes.

About two months after the disastrous surgery, he coaxed Sharon into visiting the archery range at Canandaigua's Creekside Gun Shop. He put her modified bow in her hands and nudged her toward the firing line.

"When I walked up there, everybody kind of conveniently disappeared," Sharon remembered with a laugh. "I could hear them moving out of the way."

Aiming in the darkness with Tim's guidance, Sharon sent her arrow toward a paper turkey target.

"I killed that turkey," she said. "I sometimes wonder what would have happened if I had missed it."

But she didn't miss, so she kept on shooting and hitting the target.

Tim tinkered with various sighting devices, and ultimately settled on an aluminum tube with a bead on the front and a V-notch on the back end. He moved it up and down the bow limb until he was able to line up a target perfectly from behind his wife's shoulder.

With each practice session, Sharon's shooting improved.

After a few weeks of consistent bull's eyes, she began to think it might be possible to hunt again, after all.

When fellow members of New York Bowhunters Inc. told her about the Pennsylvania-based Physically Challenged Bowhunters of America, she joined that organization and entered a drawing for a guided Minnesota deer hunt which was open to disabled archers, only.

"I was lucky enough to have my name drawn," said Pagel.

In October, Sharon and 24 other bowhunters spent a week pursuing whitetails with their guides at a 4,000-acre Minnesota Boy Scout camp.

Some of the hunters were amputees and shot one-handed, with bows braced against their chests. Others hunted in wheelchairs. Sharon was one of five blind archers in the group. Only one participant in the hunt, a paraplegic, bagged a deer, but nobody went home empty-handed.

"It was a week of laughing and talking and joking and doing all the things these hunters used to do before they became disabled," Sharon said. "It was just wonderful."

When New York's Southern Zone archery season opened in mid-October, she was raring to go.

Tim, who works for Kodak in Rochester, purchased two 10-foot-high ladder stands that could be erected side-by-side against a sturdy tree trunk.

"I'm one of those people who gets nervous six inches off the ground," Sharon said. "That's one of the few advantages of being blind. I can't look down."

Although she estimates she killed more than 50 deer in 55 years of hunting with firearms, Sharon had never loosed an arrow in three previous seasons of bowhunting.

By early November, two deer had come near the Pagels' stand, but not close enough to shoot.

"I was starting to resign myself that this was going to be another one of those years," she said.

Then, on the next-to-last Sunday of the season, she

finally got her chance.

After Sharon shot the buck, she and Tim waited quietly in their stand for half an hour. If the deer was wounded, they wanted it to lie down close by. Quick pursuit might cause it to run a great distance in panic.

As it turned out, Tim and Jeff found the dead whitetail less than 100 yards away. Sharon's arrow had pierced its lungs, resulting in a quick kill.

"When Tim led me to the deer, the first thing I did was get down on my knees beside it and say thank you," she said.

Then she gutted her buck, with help from Tim, just like she used to.

"It wasn't the neatest job, but I managed," she said.

She posed proudly with the deer as Tim and Jeff clicked away with the family camera. Later Tim discovered he had forgotten to load the film.

"My first deer with a bow and we don't have a single picture," Sharon said.

Since her return to the field, Sharon has become an enthusiastic advocate for physically challenged hunters.

When New York Bowhunters Inc. held its annual three-day rendezvous in LeRoy last month, she was a featured speaker. She urged her listeners to push themselves to do their best.

"If there's one thing I can't stand it's to have somebody say 'I can't,'" she said. "There isn't anything you can't do if you want to do it badly enough.

"Somewhere down deep inside all of us is the strength

to go on and do the things we think are impossible. I found that strength and I know you can, too."

After telling her story, she stepped outside and fired three arrows into a four-inch circle at 20 yards.

"Tim and I make a great team," she told her audience. "And since we're a team, if I happen to miss, I can always say it's his fault."

She couldn't stay long, she apologized. She was scheduled to take part in a tractor pull later that afternoon – as a driver.

ROCKER KEEPS 'EM REELING
April 1, 1993

Ted Nugent, the rock 'n' roll bowhunter, was taking aim at his favorite targets, and scoring a string of gleeful bull's eyes.

"MTV is on me right now to produce a hunting special," Nugent told his lunch companions at the OnCenter. "MTV! Now you don't think those folks need to hear the truth, do you?"

He bit into a cheeseburger with the works and then launched into another salvo.

"I'm the first guy ever that can really make the antis squirm," he said.

Nugent rattled off the list of talk-show arenas where he has wrestled with representatives of the Fund for Animals, People for the Ethical Treatment of Animals and other anti-hunting "Gomers," as he calls them. "Donahue." "Sally Jesse Raphael." "Sonya Live."

The outcome always is the same, he boasted. Before the credits roll, Ol' Tedley, Teditor the Predator, is standing over his glassy-eyed quarry. Cleveland Amory, the essayist, critic and founder of the Fund for Animals, is one of Nugent's favorite Gomer trophies.

"On 'Sonya Live,' I *pummeled* Cleveland Amory," he said. "I reduced him to a quivering pile of snot and hair. He couldn't put five words together, he was so rattled."

Ostensibly, Nugent was in Syracuse for a Landmark

Theatre performance by his band, Damn Yankees. But he spent most of the day in his unofficial role as bowhunting's crusading knight errant.

Before lunch on concert day he jousted with three area radio DJs and called a half-dozen stations in other cities to set up interviews during future tour stops.

Then he donned zebra-striped cap and camouflage vest to attend the Syracuse Outdoor Sports Show with Jim Froio, the New York state director of his 12,000-member bowhunting organization, Ted Nugent World Bowhunters Inc. For three hours, he signed autographs for fans who filed past the Taylor Outfitters booth.

"You bowhunt?" he asked one teenager. "That's not *too* much fun, is it? Sure beats hanging out at the mall."

At 4 p.m., Nugent trotted downstairs to a seminar room. With evangelical fervor, he exhorted hunters to stand tall against those who would ban their sport and urged youngsters to resist the pull of those old rock 'n' roll demons, drugs and alcohol.

An hour later, he reluctantly excused himself to get ready for his concert.

Nugent is a man on a mission.

Ever since he first hit the top of the charts in the early 1970s with hits like "Cat Scratch Fever," the Jackson, Mich., guitar player-singer has been touting the virtues of hunting and the evils of drugs to his audiences.

Nugent took up both guitar and bow at the age of 8. As he grew older, one instrument took him to some dark doorsteps, but the other always guided him back.

"When it came time to make pivotal, life-survival

decisions, the things I learned from hunting enabled me to spit in the faces of my peers who claimed I was out of touch because I didn't do drugs," he said.

He remembered other rockers who made fun of his passion.

"Jimi Hendrix," he said. "He was such a great guitar player ... all the rest of us looked up to him, I literally worshipped the ground he walked on, but he laughed at me because I hunted and asked how I could kill those poor, defenseless animals.

"Then he said, 'Here, take some of this LSD because it will help you play the guitar better.' Six months later he was dead. He gagged on his own vomit. Now, that's really hip."

"I could list you 50 other rock 'n' rollers who thought I was funny because I hunted, and they're all dead. They're dead from drugs, squirming in the grave, but I'm still up there, 44 years old and kicking butt."

Nugent says he has never tried drugs nor even taken a drink of alcohol. But staying clean and physically fit isn't the only reason he hunts.

The Nugent family – an all-American assemblage of archers what include his wife, Shemane, and another four children, ages 8 to 22, who Ozzie and Harriet would be proud to adopt – never buys meat at the store.

"The only meat we eat is what we shoot," Nugent said.

On any given night the entrée might be wild turkey with curry sauce, wild boar chops or venison Stroganoff. The recipes are included in Nugent's book, "Blood Trails: the Truth About Bowhunting."

"In my state, half a million hunters and their families ate 27 million pounds of venison last year," Nugent said. "What are you going to do, tell them all of a sudden they have to do without that food?"

And what about the carnage on the highway?

"We had 70,000 deer-car crashes in Michigan last year, and 12 people were killed in those crashes," he said. "If you banned hunting, you wouldn't have 12 casualties, you'd have 120."

He also speaks of the "spirituality" of hunting, of the closeness between predator and prey.

Yet the essence of his devotion, Nugent said, is so personal that nobody, save other hunters, can truly understand.

"People don't hunt to put backstraps in the freezer, they don't hunt because they want to get out of the office, they don't hunt to manage game animals," Nugent said. "They hunt because there's something inside them. It's called instinct."

That's nothing to be shamed of; in fact, it's something to be proud of, he insists.

"Let's get past this paranoia we have," he told his sports show listeners. "We hunters don't just harvest, we kill stuff. If we don't kill it, we can't grill it. But make sure you remind your non-hunting neighbors that somebody killed the meat they eat, too."

Such tough talk has made him some enemies.

Anti-hunters, Nugent said, repeatedly have threatened to kill him and members of his family. At the OnCenter, he warned would-be assassins that he'll be "armed and ready" if they try it.

He scowled at the thought of some fellow hunters – mainly outdoor writers, he said – who have suggested his aggressive proselytizing is doing more harm than good.

Nugent calls his friendly detractors "the dispassionate, monotone, so-called leadership of the hunting fraternity."

"If those guys are my representatives, then I'd better take up golf," he said. "They've willfully limited themselves to preaching to the choir. I want them to get out of the way so I can reach people."

Nugent's celebrity status opens doors that are closed to other defenders of sportsmen's rights.

Two weeks ago, for example, he dialed Rush Limbaugh and stayed on the air with the nation's most listened-to radio talk show host, for a full half hour. Afterward, Nugent gave Limbaugh a mounted deer head. The 8-pointer, which Nugent arrowed in Michigan, can be seen nightly on the set of Limbaugh's TV program, looking over the host's shoulder.

"I'm going to go where no other sportsmen have tried to go," Nugent said. "I'm hunting virgin territory, and Gomers are in sight and there are no bag limits."

IT'S A COYOTE, AND A FEW MORE ANSWERS
December 26, 2004

One of the perks of being the outdoors writer for a large metropolitan daily, as one of my former editors liked to describe The Post-Standard, is the opportunity to talk and correspond with good people who share a love for hunting and fishing.

I enjoy reading the letters and e-mails – most of them, anyway.

The phone calls are welcome, too, although I must admit some of the subjects come up so often they fall into the category of golden oldies.

Take the message someone left on my answering machine the other day, for example.

"I was driving from Marcellus to Syracuse when this big, furry, brownish animal ran across Seneca Turnpike," the caller said. "Could it possibly have been a wolf?"

The answer to that question, and the several others like it I get most years, is no. I am 99.99 percent certain that all such callers are seeing not wolves, but coyotes. Wolves have been absent from New York for more than a century, while coyotes are now common in every county north of the Bronx.

The wolf query made me think of some of the other questions that I field on a fairly regular basis. Maybe answering them in this space will save a few readers the trouble of dialing me up in 2005:

How come there are no deer anymore in the place where I hunt? This one, or some version of it, comes up every year between Thanksgiving and Christmas.

Chances are the hunter on the other end of the line has been sitting on the same stump beside the same trail for the last 20 years, while everything else in the neighborhood, including the location of deer food sources and bedding areas, has gradually changed. Then again, deer numbers in the caller's neighborhood might be down significantly due to over-hunting, habitat loss or the after-effects of a harsh winter.

If I were dishonest, the most ingratiating response I could give would be "it's the state's fault." That's what the disappointed hunter is thinking.

What happened to all the pheasants? Ring-necked pheasants used to nest in every grassy, overgrown farm field in Central New York. Since the early 1970s, however, most of those fields have been plowed under to make room for big, expensive houses or ankle-deep crops such as soybeans or alfalfa.

Where can I take my kid to catch a few fish? There are dozens of good spots in Central New York, but if somebody living in or near Syracuse asks for a can't-miss location in May, June or July, I usually refer them to Onondaga Lake Park, which teems with small to medium-size bluegills.

When does the trout (or bass, walleye, etc.) season start (or end)? Frankly, this one always makes me shake my head. The season dates are listed in the "Fishing Regulations Guide" that's handed out, free of charge, with every new fishing license. If the caller can't take a moment to look up the pertinent season, how likely is it that he or she will worry about creel limits or legal fishing methods?

I'm planning to go deer hunting Monday and was wondering if you knew of any hunter education classes this weekend?

People who procrastinate this long are out of luck. The state requires first-time license buyers to take a Department of Environmental Conservation-approved training course, but the dozens of such sessions held in the Syracuse area each fall are over by mid-November.

Have they stocked my creek yet? This query is common in April, when trout season is just getting underway. If the stream in question is in Onondaga County, I refer to the latest stocking report from the local Carpenter's Brook Fish Hatchery, but if the water flows elsewhere, I point the caller toward the appropriate regional DEC office.

Can you recommend a fishing guide to me? The answer depends on where the caller is headed. I never recommend a guide I haven't fished with. If possible, I'll recommend a couple of guides, to give the reader a choice.

Where can I go hiking in the fall without getting shot by hunters? My reply is, anywhere you like to hike in the spring, summer or winter. Just take the common-sense precaution of wearing a Blaze Orange jacket, vest or cap, so that you can be readily seen at a distance.

It must be great to get paid to go hunting and fishing all of the time, huh? My stock answer is, yes, it must be great. Unfortunately, I get paid for writing about hunting and fishing. That's pretty neat in its own way, but the truth is, many readers spend more time than I do with rod or gun in hand, which is one reason I enjoy talking to them so much.

A REWARDING DAY
November 1, 2001

Intrigued by Dave Odell's come-hither quacking, a lonesome duck flew toward our raft of decoys, and we leaned forward, shotguns at the ready.

But instead of dropping by for a visit, the drake made a sharp right turn and then parachuted into a flock of fellow mallards in the middle of the St. Lawrence River.

The bird's swift departure prompted Odell to make a suggestion.

"I wonder if they're being spooked by your blind," the Department of Environmental Conservation's Region 8 wildlife manager said. "It's really flapping in the breeze."

Cayuga resident Tim Noga and I were sharing a portable cloth blind adjacent to the reed-covered, wood-framed structure occupied by Odell, Jordan resident Keith DePauw and Wayne Radley of Auburn.

"Well, why don't we move and find out?" Noga responded. "It's worth a try."

Odell is an expert waterfowler, and it usually pays to heed his advice.

Ten minutes after Noga and I had folded our blind and settled into a new hiding place in a stand of cattails, Radley downed a mallard. And shortly after that, a Canada goose was added to the bag.

When birds are scarce and each shot counts, little things

can make a big difference.

The evening before, we had anticipated a day of fast action. Bands of lake-effect snow whistled across the Tug Hill Plateau and a chilly rain tattooed the motel windows. Duck hunters welcome such nasty weather because it tends to keep migratory flocks flitting from bay to bay.

Unfortunately, conditions had changed overnight.

As we crept down the steep riverbank and began setting out our decoys, the river was illuminated by twinkling stars. A stiff northwest wind blew a froth of whitecaps across the shallow bay, but the rain had stopped, and when the sun came up it was framed by patches of blue sky.

Ducks flew now and then, but in small squadrons, instead of the feathered regiments we'd seen in our dreams.

"These birds act like they've been hunted before," Odell observed.

Most likely they were local nesters, rather than fresh arrivals from Canada. The majority of the ducks we spotted stayed well beyond the 40-yard stake that Radley had hammered into the river bottom as a range marker.

Between shots, which is most of the time, duck hunters occupy themselves by admiring the scenery, talking and eating, though not necessarily in that order.

The view on the upper St. Lawrence always is compelling. As we rigged our decoys, three sea-going vessels sat in the main channel. With their deck lights aglow, they looked more like floating casinos than carriers of oil and grain. They chugged west toward Lake Ontario soon after dawn.

Although few swung close enough to merit a volley, a

variety of waterfowl species flew over the river during the morning. Judging by their wing beats and silhouetted shapes, the majority were mallards and geese, but we also watched several long lines of brant skimming just above the foamy currents.

Three times a great blue heron glided over our blinds, so close we might have been able to touch it with outstretched hands.

"He must really be used to humans," Radley noted.

Or perhaps he was simply annoyed with us for intruding on a favorite fishing spot.

When we pulled the decoys and trudged back up the hill at noon our combined bag consisted of two mallards, a black duck and a goose, far less than the 30 ducks and 10 geese permitted to our party under state and federal law.

Nevertheless, it had been a rewarding day.

Along with the Thousand Islands vistas and plenty of good conversation, DePauw could savor some nice water work by his Chesapeake Bay retriever, Katie.

Most important, every bird in the bag had died quickly and cleanly. Because we had taken no shots out of range, there were no cripples to weigh on our consciences or spoil the taste of our game.

"DEER DIARY: YOU'LL NEVER BELIEVE…"
November 24, 1994

In 25 years of examining white-tailed deer shot by New York hunters, Department of Environmental Conservation senior wildlife biologist Mike Hall has seen everything from antlered does to a unicorn.

But just when he thinks he's reviewed the complete catalog of deer deformities, diseases and predicaments, some hunter gives him a surprise.

One of the strangest was the buck that had 30 feet of wire wound tightly around its antlers.

"It appeared to be electric-fence wire," said Hall, who ages and weighs hundreds of whitetails annually at freezer plants and roadside check stations for the DEC. "We guessed that the deer somehow got hung up on a fence and escaped by rolling up the whole strand of wire on his horns."

The hunter who showed the buck to Hall a few years ago at the state's deer-check station south of LaFayette said he planned to mount the antlers just as he first saw them, wire tiara and all.

A deer's curiosity is a pathway to all sorts of entanglements.

Tom Gregg, a DEC senior wildlife technician who usually works the check station detail with Hall, said his colleague's story reminded him of the doe that died with a beer ball on its head.

The DEC's deer-check station was always good for a few stories, some of them true but stranger than fiction.

An Oswego County bowhunter arrowed the animal in 1991. Biologists figured the doe had been wearing the weird chapeau for about three weeks by that time. Eventually it would have starved to death, if not for the archer's act of mercy.

"The best explanation we could come up with was that the beer ball had been filled with some kind of food," Gregg recalled. "Possibly it was a hanging bird feeder. Somehow the deer managed to poke its head through a hole in it and then couldn't get the thing off."

Instead of a hat, Geneva resident Jim Menotti's 1993 buck wore a bracelet.

As he field-dressed the 6-pointer, Menotti noticed a 2-inch-wide, red band around its right foreleg. The hard plastic object turned out to be a screw-on rim from a flashlight. It was so tightly fitted that Menotti couldn't pry it loose.

Apparently the animal had stepped through the ring months earlier and had been unable to work its hoof free.

Compared to happenings like that, antlered does are almost common.

Hall and his co-workers at the check station see a doe with horns on its head about once every other year. C.W. Severinghaus, a retired DEC biologist, estimated New York's deer herd holds about one antlered doe for every 2,000 antlered bucks.

Typically, a doe with horns owes her adornment to a hormone deficiency. Antler growth is triggered by the pituitary gland, in response to changing periods of daylight. Most does have hormones that repress the signal to sprout antlers.

As antlers develop, they are coated with a soft skin called velvet. Bucks shed their velvet in the fall, but antlered does keep theirs until the horns drop off in early winter, Hall explained.

"I've never seen an antlered doe without velvet," he said.

Slightly less rare are piebald deer.

Piebald means "blotchy" or "spotted." While at least 99 out of 100 deer sport gray-brown coats in autumn, a piebald deer has noticeable white patches on its hair.

"Like a paint horse," Gregg said.

A doe with horns or a buck with unusual coloration has no trouble making its way in the wild kingdom, but it's a wonder some of the other deer biologists examine each fall survived until their first hunting season.

"One guy brought a blind deer to the check station," Hall remembered. "It was born blind. It was 5 or 6 months old when it was shot and seemed go be in good condition except for the fact it couldn't see."

That's the only blind deer he's checked, but Hall examines at least one three-legged deer every autumn.

"And I'm not talking about a deer which had its leg shot off recently," he said. "We've checked quite a few deer which had healed stumps from injuries that occurred long before."

Most of these amputations are the result of run-ins with farm equipment when deer are fawns, rather than hunters' poor shooting.

Among the other whitetail maladies that arrive annually at the check station are ugly-but-harmless fibroma tumors, bald spots caused by eczema or mange; and under-slung jaws due to recessive genes.

Not only odd deer, but unusual hunters as well, build up a biologist's treasure of memories.

On a couple of occasions, Hall said, he has opened a deer's mouth to find a bough of pine or hemlock tucked inside.

"Every time, those deer were shot by hunters who came over recently from Europe," Hall said. "It's an old custom of theirs to put a sprig in the deer's mouth as a sign of respect for the life they've taken."

And then there was the hunter who pulled up at the check station to have his deer weighed, innards and all.

"He was a greenhorn who had no idea he was supposed to gut the deer before dragging it out of the woods," Hall said. "I guess he thought the butcher would do it."

Now, what about that unicorn?

Hall admitted it wasn't really a unicorn, at all, but a whitetail that had a third antler between the usual pair of left-right beams.

"Right out of the center of its forehead," Hall said. "I guess it was more of a deer-corn than a uni-corn."

FULFILLMENT FLOWS FROM NEAREST STREAM
March 22, 1996

Hi, my name is Mike, and I'm a troutaholic.

I'm addicted to trout fishing. Obsessed. Hooked.

Here's how wretched I've become:

Every year about mid-March, when "The Quiet Man" is running nightly on at least three stations and the six-packs of Guinness Stout have moved up to the front row in the supermarket beer coolers, I have The Dream.

In The Dream, which will be re-run on my internal viewing screen several times between now and April 1, the opening day of trout season, I am wading Nine Mile Creek and catching fish, one after another. These are big, slob browns and crimson-bellied brook trout, rainbows with tails as wide as snow shovels and chinook salmon so heavy I can't lift them from the water.

Yeah, I know. There are no rainbow trout in Nine Mile Creek unless the hatchery truck has made a wrong turn, and never any chinooks. And fish aren't the only things out of place in The Dream.

When I fish in my sleep, Nine Mile doesn't necessarily flow north from Otisco Lake, as the map says. In Dream Land, the creek often meanders east or west, right down the middle of Main Street in Marcellus. Pools that were wiped away years ago by floods or highway excavations magically reappear in place of the pavement next to

Nojaim's market or in front of the Village Tavern.

I figure this weirdness is a psychedelic thing, sort of a trout-induced flashback.

It's also a warning that I need a fishing fix, and soon. April can't get here fast enough.

Now, if you're thinking that perhaps this little hobby of mine has gotten out of control and I should just give it up, forget it. I've tried to do without, year after year.

Trout season ends on Sept. 30 in most waters, but the state attempts to keep the lid on hardcore addicts by letting them feed their habits in a few streams year-round. The idea is that we can dry out gradually between our seasonal angling orgies instead of going cold turkey, but the concept is a cruel joke in wintry Central New York.

Is there a more pitiable sight than the poor fisherman

Author creeps into casting position on one of his favorite small streams.

who wanders along the banks of an ice-encrusted brook in February, looking desperately for just one patch of open water?

Non-anglers and even most other fishermen have a hard time figuring what makes trout junkies tick.

It's definitely not the size of the quarry. Tackle store stories aside, our favorite fish seldom grow big enough to cover a frying pan, head to tail.

Nor can we point, with any sincerity, to the contemplative aspects of the sport. Those high-toned essays Izaak Walton and other library anglers have penned about trout fishing should be taken with a generous dose of laxative.

Devotees of other species do much of their casting and catching from boats, between sips of tall cool ones. Trout fishermen aren't so leisurely. They spend quality time crawling on hands and knees through alder thickets and leap-frogging to dime-size boulders, while a forgotten thermos of coffee grows cold in the truck.

We are probably never more pathetic, as a group, than on April Fool's Day, when we spring from our cozy beds at dawn to fish in runoff flows that have the color and warmth of a chocolate Slurpee.

But the bug is not altogether unpleasant.

We trouters have fallen head over hip boots into a bottomless pit. Tumbling along a swift river, we see and feel and smell and taste all manner of things that can't be found anywhere else.

The fish, though small, are glittering jewels, with fins like arrows and sides decked out in Christmas lights of red, yellow and blue. Studying trout in the hand, it is awe-inspiring to realize that they have not changed appreciably in a million years and can live only in water that is clear, cold and pure.

On opening day, the hills that overlook my favorite stream are draped with white and pink trilliums. Later, when the sulfur mayflies are hatching, I find clumps of turk's cap lilies dripping with dew in the swamp edges. Bushes heavy with black raspberries are mine for the plucking in August, and purple loosestrife and jewelweed cast soft reflections on the pools and riffles by Labor Day.

Though my streamside explorations seldom splash through deep, Waltonian currents, wild water does have a way of washing the soul, and my well of troubles is always gone dry by the time I have fished downriver and back.

Trout fishing may be a drug, but it is also an incredible rush.

THE HUNT: AN ANCIENT INSTINCT
November 20, 1995

Today I run with the wolves.

Many of the half million or so hunters who will go afield this morning to open New York's Southern Zone firearms season for white-tailed deer might explain themselves in other terms, but that says it for me.

I would not take the life of a buck or doe merely to keep other deer from starving, nor to log quality time with hunting pals, nor even to save on grocery bills. All of those are beneficial effects of my quest, but none is its cause.

I hunt because I, like the wolf, am a hunter, descended from a long line of hunters.

"Take your gear, therefore, your quiver and your bow," the dying Isaac implored his son Esau in the Book of Genesis. "And go out into the country to hunt some game for me."

Since humans first climbed down from the trees, they have given chase – and been chased.

Hunger was never the main motivation, not even when cave dwellers circled woolly mammoths with rocks and clubs.

Spiritually, hunting links modern man with the ancients. It awakens half-forgotten senses, and washes the soul in a tidal wave of emotions.

I killed my first deer more than 20 years ago, but I can remember as if it were yesterday.

It was a sunny, chilly morning, the second day of the season. I had overslept, and it was past 8 o'clock when I drove around a bend on a country road and saw two large dogs tracing playful circles in a frost-covered field.

On second look, they were not dogs, but deer. A buck with a gleaming white rack was panting after a doe, oblivious to my parked vehicle.

I put the car in park, drew my double-barreled LeFever from the back seat without bothering to turn off the ignition, and stepped off the road, dropping two slugs in the chambers as I walked.

When the buck ran by, 50 or 60 yards distant, I squeeze the right trigger, then the left.

At the echoing blasts, both deer bounded south across the field and disappeared in a sprawling stand of hardwoods. My hands were trembling as I plucked the empty hulls from the shotgun. I knew I had missed and would probably never see that buck again, but I resolved to follow its track anyway, just in case.

After locking the car, I hurried to the spot where the buck had been when I fired. There was no hair on the ground, no speck of blood to indicate a wound, but two sets of prints, dark indentations in the whitened meadow, looked easy to follow.

I tried to stalk in silence, but the alfalfa crunched loudly beneath my boots. Still, I crept along, eyes up, and paused every few seconds to listen. Just inside the woods, I heard a footstep softer than my own. Freezing in place, I sorted through the shadows to pinpoint the shuffling sound.

It was the same buck, tip-toeing straight toward me. No doubt he was looking for his lost love.

When the 8-pointer was so close I could see the breath curling from his nostrils, I slowly raised my shotgun, covered his white chest with the muzzle, and fired. The deer turned and ran through a screen of saplings and berry bushes. I heard four, maybe five bounding steps, then nothing.

A few minutes later I found him stretched out beside a rotting log, stone dead. Never before had I felt such a rush of feelings. Excitement. Panic. Relief. Regret. Wonder. Exultation. And finally, gratitude.

This surge of emotion at the climax of the hunt is what sets two-legged predators apart from their wild kin. Though the wolf's heart beats faster when it catches a whiff of whitetail on the wind, the beast brooks no pity for its prey. A pack of wolves will drag an exhausted deer to the ground and slowly eat it alive. But human hunters, save for the few who shame us all, would rather miss cleanly with their only shot of the season than condemn a wounded animal to a lingering death.

My slug had pierced the deer's heart, collapsed a lung and passed through the liver. The buck had died on its feet in seconds, with minimal suffering. Kneeling beside him, cradling his antlers in my lap, I thanked the maker – and asked his forgiveness.

Late that night, before going to bed, I studied the buck, now hung from a beam in my garage. He would feed my young family all that winter. I stood there some time, reliving my lucky hunt, then shut the door.

The stars were out, and a full moon was up. I raised my head toward the heavens, but I did not howl.

The author has his own reasons to hunt, not the least of them being his taste for tender venison.

CARNIVORES COME IN VARIOUS FORMS
February 24, 2000

Most of the correspondence I receive from readers is interesting and informative, and a surprising share of letters are so complimentary as to make me blush. Thank you for all your kind regards and contributions to intelligent discourse.

Of course, the mail box does contain the odiferous exception to the rule now and then.

The really rank stuff, amounting to no more than several letters a year, comes from ardent anti-hunters who think the likes of me should be drawn and quartered, while Bambi and Thumper cheer the executioner from the best seats in the coliseum.

Missives of this sort are usually penned in an angry, barely legible scrawl, unsigned and sporting no return address. Naturally, they get the short shrift they deserve.

On rare occasion, a rabid anti-hunter has the guts to sign his or her name. In such cases, I usually hold my nose and pen a polite reply. I respect anyone who has the courage of conviction, however misinformed.

One bold reader sent in a tear sheet of my Feb. 17 story about a rabbit-hunting contest sponsored by the Otisco Lake Rod & Gun Club.

Above my photo of a hunter holding a dead cottontail, she wrote:

"Did this rabbit attack this man? If not, why kill it? Keep cowards like this out of the paper."

Since this lady stood up for her beliefs, I shall go out on a limb for mine.

The successful rabbit hunter is no more cowardly than the fox or owl that preys on the same animal for much the same reason.

The rabbit in that photo will make a tasty and nourishing supper for the hunter and his family. Its sacrifice will postpone but not deter the consumption of some other animal – perhaps a cuddly hog or Black Angus steer – that has been raised for the market and bloodily dispatched behind the closed doors of a slaughterhouse.

Madam letter-writer, if you ever eat turkey on Thanksgiving or chow down on a Big Mac, you are morally equivalent to the hunter, admit it or not. You are both carnivores. The main difference between the two of you is that you let others do all of your butchering. The hunter prefers to gather his vittles the old-fashioned way, while reconnecting with his roots and working up a healthy sweat.

Should you happen to be a vegetarian, bless you, but don't expect me to show up at your next covered-dish supper with a bowl of bean sprouts. I like my casseroles on the chewy side.

Perhaps a basic lesson in biology is not out of order here.

One would imagine, on hearing the lamentations of anti-hunters, that all rabbits would live to a ripe old age, if only hunters would leave them alone. When each bunny's time expired, it would simply lay its head on its forepaws and go to sleep, happily ever after.

In truth, New York's licensed hunters kill upwards of 600,000 rabbits a year, without making a dent in the state's overall population of cottontails. Many more bunnies than that are killed by wild predators, roaming house cats and speeding automobiles. The scientists who study such things say no more than 15 percent of rabbits born in the wild survive until their first birthday.

Does my compassionate correspondent believe that a rabbit can tell one mode of death from another, and would hurl itself beneath a rolling set of Michelins rather than succumb to the sharp talons of a hawk or a load of number 6 shot?

The animal makes no such distinction.

I, on the other hand, firmly believe that a rabbit drumstick looks much lovelier laid upon a dinner plate than smeared across the highway.

WRITER SPEAKS VOLUMES
November 22, 2001

Because unsigned letters are the work of cowards, I normally deposit them in my circular file. However, I decided to make an exception with the following missive, in order to give interested readers a look at the thought processes of an anti-hunting zealot. The correspondent, who listed no return address, felt compelled to comment on my Nov. 15 column on why hunters hunt, as follows:

"Mr. Kelly: Glad to see you show your true colors and biases, again. Despite your ignorant, self aggrandizing proclamations, your non-hunting neighbors get it perfectly well, thank you. Here's why:

"No. 1 – we are prohibited from walking freely in the woods to enjoy nature because some gung-ho (expletive deleted) might very well blow your head off. There is a paramount safety issue pertaining to hunting and guns in America.

"No. 2 – we are not beholding and weeded to the revenues that hunting brings private industry, who support you like a paid spokesman continually blowing the praises of hunting. Some may rightly call your self-serving advocacy a form of prostitution, Mr. Kelly.

"No. 3 – the majority of non-hunters who read the sports page tire of your endless, self-praising dribble (sic) when we know there are fundamental safety and public policy gun issues which are in fact a danger to a civilized society. The cave man days are over, Tarzan!

"No. 4 – You reveal the secret male, phony machismo, great-white-hunter mentality that many of us common folk do despise. Thus, you just cannot help but show off your kill to neighbors. I have a cat who brings home dead mice and moles to show off just like you do. Remember your appeal to readers not to send in tasteless, gory pictures of dead animals! And now we read that you're "blessed" to do this. (Oh my God… does Kelly border on the lunatic fringe of the religious right, too?)

"If, as your opinion survey claims, 6 to 7 percent of Americans hunt, where do you come up with the illogical deduction of an antagonistic minority? Where I went to school that would mean 93 to 94 percent who do not hunt would be a majority, dumbbell.

"Hunt if you want to, I really don't care. But please, get off your tiresome bandwagon of all this misleading, self-serving crap you insist on perpetuating in your column. Reputable journalists are supposed to be seeks (sic) of truth, not whores for the hunting industry and weak-minded men seeking to bolster their ego. Your urges may be natural to you, but repugnant to others.

"Have a nice opening day!"

Well, that certainly speaks volumes. In fact, I couldn't have said it better, myself. Thanks for taking the time to write.

And in case you're wondering, opening day wasn't half bad. I was blessed, for sure, to bag a 3-point buck, which netted 60 pounds of boned meat for the family freezer.

THE BEST PART OF FISHING? PASSING ON THE TRADITION
March 21, 2000

Seeing Westdale fly-tier Allen Fannin on the cover of this section reminded me of my own fishing mentors, and the responsibility which all anglers share to pass on the skills and traditions of their sport.

As usual, Fannin is surrounded by curious kids. One of them, Sam Morse of Camden, is a true prodigy who won a roomful of trophies at regional and national fly-tying contests after learning the basics from Fannin. The other two, Kazia Clanton and Justin Crosby of Syracuse, have just taken their first steps down the fishing path. How far they go may depend on the encouragement they receive from other anglers.

As a certified instructor for the 4-H Sportfishing and Aquatic Resources Education Program (SAREP), Fannin has helped hundreds of kids to catch a bluegill or tie a Royal Coachman. He's also taught fly-tying and fly-casting to many eager adults.

He is generous with his time in part because so many other fishermen were willing to share their secrets with him.

As a 10-year-old living in Brooklyn, Fannin used to take the bus to the Patterson Casting Club in New Jersey, where he practiced his roll casts and double hauls with Joan Salvato. A national casting champ, Salvato eventually

The late Allen Fannin, left, of Westdale, was rightly proud of teaching more than 500 kids how to fish or tie flies.

married outdoor writer Lee Wulff and became a widely honored writer and fishing instructor, herself.

Fannin learned to tie flies during summer sessions at the state's Camp DeBruce in the Catskills. His teacher was a state game warden, Roy Steenrod, who had studied the feather and fur craft at the elbow of Theodore Gordon.

Most angling historians credit Gordon, a writer who lived along the Neversink River in the early 1900s, with popularizing dry-fly fishing in the United States. Something of a recluse, Gordon shared his fly-tying methods with only one other person, Steenrod. Imagine the loss to our heritage if that particular friendship had not blossomed!

My primary angling mentor was my father. I vividly

recall the time Dad put me on his back and waded across a runoff channel to get to the point of a narrow peninsula in Nine Mile Creek. My first brook trout grabbed a worm in that pool.

Dad was the best bait fisherman I ever knew, and in his 50s he became an excellent fly-fisher, too, after he saw some of the trout that I'd caught on artificial nymphs. Along with stream-reading and casting skills, he imparted a strong sense of ethics and sportsmanship, and I still feel compelled to report to him when the trout are hitting, even though it has been more than six years since his passing.

The father-son exchange is the classic model of angling mentorship, and I was extremely pleased last year when my own son jumped back into trout fishing with both feet after several seasons away from the water. But there are many other kinds of relationships between angling teachers and pupils, as well.

These days, fishing recruits are increasingly likely to be women, motivated to take up rod and reel by a spouse or boy friend.

Vicki Lane, the LaFayette resident who lent her expertise to another article in this issue, was initiated into fly-fishing by her husband, Mike. Since then, she has coached dozens of other women, in long-rod classes sponsored by Trout Unlimited or local tackle shops.

Along with my son, I've introduced several friends and relatives to fishing. On two occasions, I drew the names of brothers-in-law in our family's annual Christmas gift lottery. John and Bill each wound up with their first fly rod, as a result. I expect to see both of them, bright and early, on the opening day of the new trout season.

Good mentors never stop learning, themselves, and I was recently blessed with a gift of knowledge from an unexpected source.

Carl Hier of Westvale was an old friend who died a little over a year ago. Before his legs began to fail him, he and his wife Helen fished Nine Mile Creek between Marcellus Falls and Martisco nearly every day of the season. Like me, Carl was primarily a nymph fisherman, but so good at it that his fly rod seldom went more than a few minutes without curling into a deep bend.

Several months after Carl's death, Helen presented me with two fly boxes, stuffed with nymphs he had tied himself. I was overwhelmed by the bequest, for more reasons than one.

Although Carl and I had both made big dents in Nine Mile's trout population over the years, it was astonishing to see how much his collection of nymphs differed from mine. Where my flies were predominantly dark brown or tan, his were mostly gray or olive. Many of mine have bodies of seal's fur, while his pet patterns derived their living appearance from windings of ostrich plumes.

I plan to give the new flies a workout this season, and if they're as good as they look, I'll make a point of sharing them with my friends.

FAREWELL, OLD GIRL
December 4, 2005

On Nov. 18, the final day of the local pheasant season, I tumbled a nice cockbird that erupted from a patch of goldenrod with my English springer spaniel in hot pursuit.

When the rooster hit the ground, Harley pinned it in place with one paw, just like she'd always done, and look proudly in my direction, as if to ask, "How'd I do, boss?"

By my reckoning, she did just fine.

Guiding Light Harley, named after a soap opera character, was the best hunting partner I ever had. She was a beloved family member and a loyal protector with lots of bark and no bite.

On Tuesday, Harley died in my arms.

Dr. Stephen Bruck, a Marcellus veterinarian with a deep well of compassion, administered the fatal needle at my request. I wept convulsively, and that night I lay awake, thinking how quickly 13 years had passed.

My wife, Chickie, and I picked Harley from a litter of pups born in May 1992, in Vestal. I liked her black and white markings and the plucky way she climbed over her siblings to greet visitors.

The day we took her home, Chickie drove and I held the whining puppy against my chest. In that brief time, we bonded forever.

Under my wife's guidance, Harley quickly learned to sit, stay and come, but her obvious intelligence did not deter her from mischief.

Like most puppies, she liked to chew on dangling fingers and wooden furniture legs, so we sought to channel the habit by giving her our daughter Brenna's discarded cloth hand puppet, which at the time looked like a cartoon mouse.

Although the puppet was quickly chewed beyond recognition, Harley continued to play with it constantly, and we soon referred to it as her security blanket or simply, "blankey." Even in her old age, Harley would fetch that odd, stinky toy to show our houseguests.

When Harley wasn't trotting around with blankey in her mouth, she was apt to be boxing with our late cat, Tabby. They often sparred in the family room, Tabby lying on her back and flicking jabs in the air while Harley circled her, darting and barking. It was a hoot to watch.

If Harley could be a bit of a clown at home, she was deadly serious in the field. She was barely five months old when she flushed her first pheasant, a left-over from a summer field trial at the Three Rivers Wildlife Management Area. There were hundreds more birds after that one.

If Harley had any significant weakness as a hunter, it was her unwillingness to retrieve, which I always attributed to the sharp peck on the nose a wounded rooster gave her during her rookie year afield. Ever thereafter, instead of picking up a shot bird, she'd simply hold it down or stand by it until I collected it myself.

That flaw aside, she was a hunting machine. She had a radar nose, the stamina of a marathon runner and indescribable determination. She quartered instinctively, seldom ranging more than 25 or 30 yards in front of me, and promptly changed directions when I whistled or signaled left or right with my outstretched hand.

Once I realized Harley knew more about pheasants than I did, I simply tagged along, shotgun at the ready, while she slashed through fields like a canine Grim Reaper.

The number of pheasants Harley accounted for in her career was impressive, and might have been astronomical if not for my absentmindedness. One night when Harley was 2 years old, I let her out to do her duty and then simply forgot about her. An hour later there was a knock on the door and a stranger asked if we owned a black and white dog.

The car that struck Harley broke her pelvis and smashed her right hip. After emergency surgery, she underwent femoral head-and-neck surgery, a procedure in which her hip socket was essentially sawed off. Months later she was back harassing pheasants, a little slower than she used to be but even more determined.

Harley hit her peak at age 8, like most flushing dogs, but kept on ticking into her pre-teens. It was only this fall that she slowed appreciably.

During her preseason runs, Harley tripped and fell several times and occasionally ran with her right rear leg held inches off the ground. In addition, she suddenly grew hard of hearing.

I kept her subsequent workouts short. Since she could no longer hear my commands, I took care to hunt where I could watch her at all times.

It seemed her career was coming to an end, but on an early November visit to a Southern Tier shooting preserve Harley performed like a champ, flushing seven of eight birds stocked before our hunt.

On that season-ending junket at Three Rivers, my tough little buddy did so well that I began to think she had one more year in her.

Those dreams were dashed the day before Thanksgiving. That afternoon Harley didn't eat her dinner – the first time we could remember her refusing anything remotely edible. She barely lapped her water and had labored breathing.

Dr. Bruck's gentle hands detected an enlarged liver, and the veterinarian also informed us that Harley was feverish and seriously dehydrated. He wanted to keep her a couple of days to administer fluids and antibiotics, intravenously. At first he was hopeful, but on the sixth day he called us to the clinic.

Harley had taken a definite turn for the worse. Her skin and eyes had turned yellow. She was eating next to nothing. It was a gut-wrenching decision, but after a tearful few minutes together, we lifted Harley up onto the examining table.

Since then our house seems terribly empty. When I pull into the driveway, I half expect to hear Harley's bark, and in one corner of my eye I can still see her curled in that old green armchair.

Yet I am not going to lose myself in mourning. Come spring, my wife and I are going to start looking for another little springer spaniel with a spunky attitude and black freckles on her white chest.

She won't be Harley, but if we give our new pup half a chance, we will learn to love her, too

Rest in peace, old girl.

Harley was tuckered out but pleased with herself after a hunt at a game bird shooting preserve near Horseheads, NY.

THIS ANGLER ROLLS WITH THE LUNCHES
July 8, 1999

Most of the charter captains who have had me aboard their vessels know all too well that even a short ride across a choppy sea causes my stomach to tumble like Nadia Comaneci.

When the waves are rolling on Lake Ontario, I usually grip the gunwales, fix my eyes on shore and tell somebody else to run for the rod when a fish strikes.

A tendency toward turn-yourself-inside-out seasickness can be embarrassing for an outdoors writer, but there's no hiding it.

Bill Thomas, the former president of the Eastern Lake Ontario Salmon and Trout Association, used to invite me to join him on the group's annual summer outing, which consisted of a day of trolling near Oswego or Fair Haven followed by a Dutch-treat dinner at a nearby restaurant.

As I recall, the first time out was a lark, but the second was a sour-mouthed disaster. The fish were biting, but the lake surface was wrinkled by four-foot rollers.

Soon, sky and water alike began to bob and weave before my eyes. It was such an intoxicating sight that my lunch decided to come up for a look. My breakfast, too.

The following year Bill called me the night before our scheduled trip to inform me that the wind was expected to be pretty strong and that he would "understand" if I skipped the fishing and merely joined the gang for dinner.

Anyone who isn't feeling a pang of sympathy for me by now must be among the 10 percent of the population who, according to medical studies, never experience motion sickness. For that's what seasickness is. It's the same thing that causes kids to upchuck on long car rides and ashen-faced adults to hurry to the back of an airplane.

Experts believe the ailment results from the brain's inability to process the conflicting sensory signals it receives when the human body and the world around it are suddenly out of sync.

Whatever the cause, the symptoms are universal. A victim turns pale, if not an alien green. He or she breaks into a cold sweat, starts to salivate and finally does abdominal flip-flops.

There are all sorts of purported cures and preventatives. Thomas swears by the Sea Band, a $10 elastic band with a hard button that is designed to exert a slight pressure between the tendons on the bottom of the wrist. Practitioners of traditional Chinese medicine claim this pressure point, which they call the neikuan, controls nausea.

I'm not a believer in Sea-Bands because I happened to be wearing one when I spray-painted the hull of Bill's boat.

I do believe in Dramamine (dimenhydrinate), a motion-sickness medicine that is available over the counter in most pharmacies and supermarkets. Usually I can keep the wobblies under control by taking one pill the night before a trip and then another an hour or so before the boat shoves off.

Unfortunately, Dramamine makes some folks' eyelids a

little heavy. Don't take it in the morning if you have a long drive to the lake.

Another potent treatment, the Transderm Scop, is a tan-colored patch that is attached to the skin behind the ear. Available by prescription only, it releases the drug scopolamine, which is supposed to block the nerve pathways that stimulate nausea.

Those of us with shaky sea legs can complement the above cures with an ounce of prevention. In most instances, the symptoms of seasickness can be minimized if you sit in the center of the boat instead of fore or aft and lock your eyes on a shoreline object rather than the undulating water.

And finally, if you're tempted by the cold sodas and sub sandwiches your shipmates are passing around, remember that what goes down sometimes must come up.

A GRAND FANTASY: IF I WERE KING
December 23, 1999

Governor Pataki can have his job, as far as I'm concerned. The salary isn't bad, and the position comes with a mansion and taxpayer-funded plane rides, but none of the perks quite make up for the office-holder's need to constantly curry favor with people he can't stand.

However, if New York was a monarchy, I might be talking treason. As Mel Brooks once said, "It's good to be the king."

If I wore the crown today, heads would roll tomorrow.

For starters, there'd be no more penny-pinching on fish and wildlife programs.

New York residents have paid the same bargain-basement rates for sporting licenses since 1991. Pataki's administration tried to increase license fees this year, but the move was stymied by state legislature Democrats. As king, I wouldn't tolerate a legislature.

Before the ink was dry on my license-hike proclamation, I'd issue another decree, establishing a habitat and access stamp.

The stamp would cost $5. Revenues would go into a royal account for the improvement of living quarters for fish and wildlife, and the acquisition of public hunting and fishing access on privately owned land.

In contrast to the voluntary habitat stamp recommended by the state Conservation Council, mine would be a mandatory purchase for all who wished to hunt the king's deer or catch the king's fish.

I'd take steps to assure my subjects' safety afield, too. Henceforth, hunters would have to wear 400 inches of fluorescent orange clothing while pursuing deer, bear or upland game with firearms.

And, speaking of upland game, I'd make sure we had some. Ruffed grouse, woodcock, cottontail rabbits and the royal family's favorite bird, the ring-necked pheasant, have become much too scarce during New York's long flirtation with democracy.

The new habitat and access stamp would generate about $7 million or $8 million in revenues annually. Each year, I'd distribute a healthy share of the fund to land owners, to plant grassy fields for pheasant nesting and clear-cut small wood lots to benefit grouse, bunnies and woodcock.

I'd also expand production at the royal pheasant farm in Tompkins County. It's shameful that New York raises only 25,000 adult pheasants a year, and that the state recently snubbed tax-paying hunters by opting to close one of its two ringneck hatcheries. The neighboring Commonwealth of Pennsylvania stocks about 200,000 pheasants annually. No king would settle for second-best.

Because New York has fewer hunters than it used to, those who continue to go afield during my reign would shoulder greater responsibility for managing the royal herd of whitetails. I'd give each licensed hunter the right to kill two bucks annually. However, the second buck could not be slain unless a doe was harvested, first.

Department of Environmental Conservation biologists suggested a similar management strategy last year, but desk-bound bureaucrats spiked the proposal. We royals don't bother with bureaucrats.

Fisheries would not be neglected during the era of King Mike, either.

A large chunk of the habitat and access fund would be spent to construct new pools in eroded trout streams and build boat launches and fishing piers on neglected New York lakes.

Fishing seasons would be lengthened but creel limits would be reduced for most species, to spread our angling wealth among as many anglers as possible.

I'd impose heavy-duty fines on salmon snaggers and other fishing law violators. And, if fines didn't do the trick, we could always dust off the rack.

There's more to this fantasy, but his Majesty has just run out of space.

BROOKIES ARE STILL THE FINEST PRIZE
March 31, 2006

For many angling families, the opening day of trout season is rooted in ritual, and when I was young that glorious occasion was not complete until my father had spread a newspaper and laid out his catch for his seven children to see.

Dad would withdraw those speckled beauties from his wicker creel, one by one, and set them down on the cellar steps with audible thumps. Many years later, I can clearly recall the cool touch and the clean smell of those trout, and the way their silvery scales stuck to the newsprint.

What I remember most about those long-ago days, however, is the way my father admired some fish more than others. Although his catch usually included at least one brown trout of impressive dimensions, Dad spent the greater part of his annual show-and-tell performances fussing over the smaller brook trout he'd landed.

Holding a 9- or 10-inch brookie before our wide eyes, he'd point out its distinctive dorsal vermiculations, the red fins edged with strips of milky white, and the rose-colored spots outlined with blue haloes.

After satisfying the curiosity of us kids, Dad usually drove up the hill and around the corner to my grandparents' house. For health reasons, Grandpa could no longer wade a swift stream, but he still looked forward to April Fool's

Day and the opportunity to give his grown son a tip or two. Like Dad, he had a soft spot for the diminutive brookies.

"Now, those are real natives," he'd say, with a fond smile.

Natives. The term stuck with me, although at first I had no idea what it meant. As I grew up and spent many joyful hours fishing for them in Nine Mile Creek and its tributaries, I gradually came to appreciate that brook trout – *Salvelinus fontinalis*, or "the char living in springs" – were called "natives" because they had thrived in the state's colder lakes and streams for eons.

Brown trout, in contrast, had been imported from Europe in the 1880s, and the rainbow trout that wax fat in several of the Finger Lakes were brought east from the Pacific Coast and the Rocky Mountains not long after that. Brookies, it seemed to me, truly belonged here; while the other species, though welcome on the end of my fishing line, were squatters.

Unfortunately, first-come does not always equate to first-served, and native brook trout have largely been supplanted by the hardier immigrants in most watersheds, not only in Central New York but throughout their original range.

When the first Europeans set foot on the North American continent, brookies filled icy streams in throughout what is now eastern Canada, New England, New York, and Pennsylvania. The species also thrived in parts of Minnesota, Michigan, Wisconsin, and the higher elevations of the Virginias, the Carolinas, Kentucky, Tennessee and northern Georgia.

Today, wild brook trout populations have dwindled in

the southern states, although restoration efforts appear to be paying off in the Great Smokies; and the species has been in a long, slow retreat in much of the Northern U.S., including New York.

In most watersheds, brookies have been forced out of main streams and into small tributaries by a succession of woes, including over-fishing and deforestation of stream banks in the late 1800s, gross water pollution and competition with brown trout through most of the 1900s, and dilution of native strains by hatchery inbreeding that continues even today.

Nine Mile Creek held so many natives in the 1950s that my father typically caught three or four of them for every brown he landed in the stream. Sadly, a massive fish kill of mysterious origins virtually eradicated the local strain of brookies in the early 1960s.

Today, brown trout dominate Nine Mile, and almost all of the so-called "natives" caught in my home water these days are hatchery graduates.

Similar stories have been written on the currents of trout streams all over the East, yet anglers who are devoted to the native species can still find wild brookies if they look hard enough.

Likely spots include any deeply shaded or spring-fed streams which are well oxygenated and have peak summer water temperatures no higher than about 66 degrees. Ideally, such waters will have high falls or other barriers that prevent brown or rainbow trout from migrating upstream and taking over the fishery.

There are dozens of streams in Oswego, Jefferson and Lewis counties that hold good size and numerous natives, and plenty more in both the Catskills and Adirondacks.

Truth be told, I know a couple of productive spots within an hour's drive of Syracuse, but don't bother to ask for directions. Brook trout streams are fragile resources, and the precise location of a good one is a secret worth taking to the grave.

Of all the fish that swim, anglers in the Kelly family love brook trout the most.

THE ART OF SEDUCTION
December 21, 2001

If the thousands of anglers who think of Oswego County's Salmon River as their second home elected a streamside government, Ed Martin would be a logical candidate to run for mayor.

The 58-year-old Boston native (he calls it BAH-stahn) has been fishing on the river since 1977, and has guided salmon and steelhead anglers for a living since the late '80s. As he rows his driftboat downstream from Altmar to Pineville on a cold December morning, half of the fishermen he passes know him by name.

"Hey, Eddie, how's it going?" "Ed, what's happening?" "Eddie, where are all the fish?"

Some of the chatty anglers are previous clients of Martin's Expert Guide Service. Others are just hoping to hook free advice from one of the river's more recognizable denizens.

It doesn't take much prodding to get Martin going on the subject of his favorite fish.

"Steelhead are really special," he said.

The rainbows that swim up the Salmon River and other Great Lakes tributaries from October through April, weeks or months in advance of their spring spawning ritual, are big, hard-fighting and hard to fool.

"You can't expect to go out for one day and be good at this game," Martin said.

Steelies, which average about 8 pounds but sometimes weigh more than 20 pounds when they return to the Salmon River, become increasingly indifferent to baits, flies and lures the longer they're hounded by anglers. Cold winter currents compound the degree of difficulty by slowing the metabolisms and diminishing the appetites of the fish.

Martin outfits his steelhead customers with long, flexible noodle rods, fly reels loaded with slender, 2- or 3-weight lines, and leaders which have a breaking strength of 4 or 5 pounds. He uses flies almost exclusively, but not just any flies.

The strong fingers that the 6-foot-2 former ironworker once used to keep a safe grip 60 stories above city sidewalks now fashion feather and fur concoctions that appear more suited to guppies than steelhead. His fly boxes are filled with egg patterns and artificial nymphs woven on tiny size 16 hooks. Most of the nymphs are tied in blue, green, yellow and orange hues, and ribbed with shiny copper wire.

"Once these fish have been tortured by fishermen for awhile, they hit small flies better than anything, even salmon eggs," he said

No bait works if it sails down the current unseen by the fish, and Martin patiently drills his clients until they master his precise method of presentation.

"I want you to cast right there," he says, pointing to the spot where a sunken limb splits the rippling river currents. "No, that one was too far downstream."

When the fly splashes down, Martin reminds his apprentice for the day to raise the rod tip sharply and keep it at a 45-degree angle throughout the drift, to maintain a tight connection between angler and fly.

"You have to get the belly out of the line, quick, he warns. "Otherwise your fly is dragging, and you won't get many fish when that happens."

Martin is dead-set against snagging or "lifting," the illegal practice of taking a fish by purposely pulling a hook point into its fin, belly or mouth instead of inducing it to bite. He came by his convictions in a roundabout way.

"I used to be a pretty good lifter, myself," he said.

Martin admits he "lifted" fish in his early years on the river "because the people in the tackle shops told me that was the only way to catch these fish, salmon and steelhead."

"Then one day I saw a guy with a rod that looked about 100 feet long and he was really whacking the fish, and catching every one of them the right way, in the mouth," he remembered. "I asked him, 'What is that thing and how do you use it?'"

It was a noodle rod, and before long Martin was using the same sort of gear to draw bites from fish that once would have snagged.

"If anyone ever gives me any bull about snagging, I can call 'em on it, because I've done it all," he said. "I know what works and what doesn't."

Now he probes the river's pools with the precision of a surgeon and plays fish with the touch of a safecracker.

"When you're using this tackle, the fish don't break you off, you break them off," he said. "You have to let them run when they want to run."

Recently he demonstrated, after concluding a float trip.

While drifting a nymph through the Cemetery Pool upstream from the Altmar bridge, he felt the line stop and set the hook on a throbbing fish.

"That's a head-shaker," he said.

As the fish began to tire, Martin applied a steady for gentle pressure by bending his rod into the shape of the letter C. Gradually he eased an Pound steelhead onto a sliver of gravel beach.

"This could be your picture fish," he said.

It was that for sure, a lovely rainbow with dark orange gill covers and black spots sprinkled along its flank. After posing for a couple of snapshots, Martin eased the trout back into the water and watched it swim away, good as new.

"What could be more beautiful than that?" he asked.

SPAWNING RAINBOWS AN APRIL CHALLENGE
April 2, 1992

Roll-casting the little Hendrickson nymph into the upper end of the run, I raised the rod tip and felt the split shot bumping along the rocky bottom of Owasco Inlet.

As the fly swept past a submerged tree stump, the line straightened. At first there was only dead weight; then the rod bowed and hummed, as the unseen fish turned and swam slowly downstream.

My first impression was of a fat white sucker, foul-hooked in the belly. The fish's ponderous moments were definitely sucker-like.

They were, that is, until the big rainbow trout at the end of my line suddenly reversed direction and somersaulted from the water.

As if to punctuate her identity, she tore straight toward the stump, and I had no choice but to lean on the rod, testing the strength of my 4-pound leader and size 14 hook.

Ultimately, the henfish lost her tug-of-war and slid back into the main current, head shaking and tail wagging. Next she decided to try the easy way out, letting the current carry her downstream, in the general direction of Owasco Lake.

Below the waist-deep run was a short stretch of rapids, and beyond that a deep pool laced with old timbers and tree limbs.

I reeled as fast as I could and sloshed downstream, trying to get to the foot of the run before the trout could reach the fast water. I made it just in time.

At 25 inches, she was the largest rainbow trout I had ever caught on a fly. Consumed with pride, I looked up and down the stream for witnesses but saw not a soul.

That great fish's portrait accompanies this article, but you will have to take my word about other triumphs on the Finger Lakes tributaries.

In the 1960s and early '70s, streams like Catharine Creek, Cold Brook and Naples Creek were flush with spawning rainbow trout each spring. The creeks drew hordes of fishermen, too, from the opening day of trout season on April 1 until early May. Some well-known pools were completely surrounded on weekends, and the Roman circus atmosphere repelled may thoughtful anglers.

In recent years, however, the old gangs have been breaking up.

Hundreds of anglers still line the banks of Catharine Creek each opening day, but fishermen who love trout and hate crowds now have long stretches of Finger Lakes tributaries to themselves after the first weekend of the season.

The Salmon River deserves most of the credit for that.

Twenty-five years ago, the Finger Lakes spring rainbow ruin afforded New York anglers their best chance, by far, to catch a trout big enough to hang on the den wall.

The state Department of Environmental Conservation broadened our trophy-fishing horizons in 1968.when it began stocking millions of trout and salmon annually in

Lake Ontario. The Salmon River and many other Ontario feeder streams in turn began to fill up with spawning steelhead trout and Chinook salmon.

In contrast to the Finger Lakes streams, which are closed Jan. 1 through March 1, the Ontario tributaries are open year-round. Some of their steelhead max out at 20 pounds or better, and the salmon are apt to be half again as hefty.

Compared to such monsters, my 25-inch Owasco Inlet trophy is a pan-fryer, and the average Finger Lakes trout of 15 inches or so is a stunted minnow. No wonder most of the old Finger Lakes rainbow-chasers now head north in the springtime.

Well, call me crazy, but I have never been bored by 15-inch trout, especially when they are my only company on a clear-flowing brook. And there's always the possibility of a bigger fish. My all-time Finger Lakes best is a 10-pound, 6-ounce beauty.

What I admire most about Finger Lakes rainbows isn't their size, but their wildness.

The sleek, black-spotted beauties finning their way up the tributaries as you read this are descended from California strains that were firmly established in Canandaiguia, Seneca, Cayuga, Owasco and Skaneateles lakes before the start of World War II.

Most of the fish you catch in these tributaries were born there. The rest are hatched by the DEC from eggs which are stripped from wild trout captured during the spawning runs.

DEC biologists say a lengthening period of daylight prompts Finger Lakes rainbows to gather off tributary mouths in late February or early March. High run-off waters then trigger the runs upstream.

The rainbows spawn in gravel-bottomed riffles when water temperatures exceed 40 degrees for a few days at a time. Afterward, the spent fish wander back to the lakes, feeding as they go.

Diaries I've kept for the past 16 years confirm that at least some big rainbows linger in the tributaries until late April. Often the fishing is excellent into the first or second week of May.

Many old-timers cling to the myth that the first big run of suckers from the lakes in April marks the end of the rainbow action. A friendly fellow repeated that old canard to me one day on Salmon Creek, the Cayuga Lake tributary five miles northeast of Ithaca. He had 10 big suckers on a stringer. I landed a bookend pair of 19-inch rainbows 50 feet from his spot, minutes after his departure.

No special expertise is required to catch tributary trout.

Although the 'bows don't feed voraciously until they've finished spawning, they can be enticed to strike egg sacks, egg-imitating chunks of orange or yellow sponge, or bright streamer flies which are drifted past their noses. The trick is to put the lure, whatever it is, right on bottom and show it patiently to a resting trout, again and again, until he is in no mood to take it any longer.

As the rainbows complete their spawning chores and begin to drop back toward the lake, they feed eagerly and can be caught easily on small garden worms.

Some of the best angling occurs when temperatures climb high enough to trigger the first mayfly hatches of the spring.

Drift a small nymph or wet fly through a deep run on a sunny April afternoon. Who knows, you might hook a 'bow even bigger than the one that made me bust my buttons with pride at the outset of this tale.

John Wall of Marcellus, NY, leads a nice Grout Brook rainbow to shore.

PAPA'S LATEST DESERVES PRAISE
July 29, 1999

"True at First Light," the latest and last of Ernest Hemingway's posthumously published works, has left a sour taste in the mouths of most reviewers.

I'm not surprised.

Never mind that Hemingway's second-eldest son, Patrick, slashed the 40-year-old original manuscript in half on its way to the publisher. The bigger barrier to the book's critical acceptance, by far, is its blatant lack of political correctness.

Given its subject, setting and secondary theme – big-game hunting, colonial Africa and the polygamous leanings of the human male – this fictionalized memoir stands little chance of getting a fair reading from today's literary establishment.

It may be up to the likes of me, therefore, to give Hemingway his due.

I'm honored to oblige. In addition to being one of the most compelling and influential novelists of any era, "Papa" Hemingway arguably was one of the greatest outdoors writers of all time.

Although much deeper themes flowed through the pages, some of the most sparkling passages in Hemingway's 1926 debut novel, "The Sun Also Rises," centered on protagonist Jake Barnes' trout-fishing getaway in Spain's

Pyrenees Mountains.

For the next three decades, Hemingway frequently honed his writing skills in wild settings.

"Big Two-Hearted River," his two-part short story about a war-weary soldier's fishing trip to Michigan's Upper Peninsula, is a classic. No angler can nibble at its spare prose without catching the scent of green ferns in his nostrils or feeling the weight of a fat brook trout in his creel.

Hemingway's genius for conveying the essence of an experience without wordy descriptions was also evident in "The Short, Happy Life of Francis Macomber," a short story about the fatal shooting of a hunter by his wife during a Kenya safari.

I have read "Macomber" a dozen times, and am still torn by the ending, as Hemingway intended. Did Mrs. Macomber do it on purpose or not?

Of course, no Hemingway retrospective would be complete without a mention of "The Old Man and the Sea," the ultimate fish story, which netted the author the Nobel Prize for Literature.

One of my personal favorites is "The Green Hills of Africa," which might now be seen as a prequel to "True at First Light."

To the world at large, Hemingway often came off as a boorish braggart. Seemingly driven to prove his masculinity in boxing ring and bedroom alike, he had four wives and periodically wandered from each.

But in "Green Hills," a semi-fictional novel based on his first African safari, Hemingway stunned me with a manly admission of weakness.

Time and again, the writer-protagonist of "Green Hills" chafes because his game trophies are smaller than those bagged by his luckier companion. Finally, after an epic chase, he kills a magnificent greater kudu, only to be outdone once more.

The writer is furious at first, then ashamed, as he recognizes the egotistical motives for his quest. As the safari draws to a close, he congratulates his rival sincerely, as a sportsman should.

The narrator of "True at First Light" is flawed, too. Midway through an extended safari, Mary Hemingway is hot on the trail of a marauding lion, but her husband's mind is elsewhere. Randy as ever, he wavers between the familiar affection he feels for Mary and the fleeting passion sparked by a young African tribeswoman.

As marital discord is about to boil over, the Hemingways suddenly find themselves in peril. Their white hunter, Philip Percival, is forced to abandon the safari temporarily to take care of pressing business at his farm, and leaves Papa in charge. The next day, word reaches camp that Mau Mau terrorists are advancing through the region, and an attack seems possible at any moment.

What happens? I'd rather have Hemingway tell you that. Nobody I know could do it any better.

HEAVEN CAN WAIT ON THE DELAWARE

May 19, 1994

A few hours before last week's solar eclipse, when most New Yorkers were wondering how they could look at the sun without damaging their eyes, Sempronious fly fisherman Joe Lora had a different concern.

"Do you think mayflies will hatch during an eclipse?" he asked

We were bouncing along Route 17 in Don Rademacher's truck, just outside of Hancock, the Catskills village where the east and west branches of the Delaware merge and turn toward the Atlantic Ocean.

"I don't know," Rademacher replied. "But I guess we're going to find out."

It would take more than a once-in-a-lifetime celestial event to keep a trio of fanatical trout anglers from an annual appointment with the Delaware's Hendrickson hatch.

The Hendrickson, Ephemerella subvaria, is a mayfly that metamorphoses from aquatic nymph to winged adult from late April into early May in Catskill-region trout streams. Hendricksons are incredibly abundant in the Delaware's sweeping rivers and, at about 10 to 12 millimeters long, big enough to ring a dinner bell for the river's largest browns and rainbows.

One of the nicest things about Hendricksons, from the angler's viewpoint, is their civilized schedule. Given normal spring conditions, they can be counted on to start hatching at about 2 o'clock each afternoon. Fishermen can sleep late, linger over brunch and still have enough time to tie some extra flies before the action starts.

If the Hendricksons were punctual this day, they would unfurl their wings in gloom. The eclipse was expected to peak at 1:28 p.m., and the moon would still be parked in front of the sun as the insects began to pop from the water.

Rademacher had miles to go before then.

The Marietta resident, who runs The Royal Coachman Ltd. Orvis shop in Skaneateles with his wife, Sandy, recently obtained his guide's license and he had invited Lora and I to join him on a shakedown trip.

We planned to launch Rademacher's wood drift boat beneath a West Branch bridge span, then fish our way down to the Pennsylvania Fish Commission's Buckingham public access on the main stem of the Delaware, near Equinunk, Pa.

The day got off to a fast start.

While Rademacher drove downriver to leave his truck at Buckingham, Lora and I baby-sat his boat and caught four pretty browns in a West Branch riffle.

"We're going to have a spectacular day," Rademacher predicted, after a friend returned him to the launch site.

As we shoved off, streamers of fog were climbing the hills along the river. Three mergansers rocketed from a boulder at the water's edge, buzzed the boat and made a wide circle before vanishing around a bend.

The West Branch flowed high and muddy after a night of showers and thunderstorms, but as we floated through the Junction Pool and on down the big Delaware the water gradually cleared, until we could see the cobble bottoms of chest-deep runs.

At midmorning, Rademacher dropped anchor where the river split and curled around three small islands.

"I call this 'The Braids,'" he said. "It's one of the best pools on the Delaware.

While Rademacher and Lora waded into the shelving riffle at the head of the pool, I waded downstream.

Near the tail of The Braids, the river has gouged a long wedge into one bank. Two swans were cruising in the side channel, hunting for snails and other snacks. They posed for the camera, ruffling their feathers and paddling almost close enough to touch.

When I went back to the boat for more film, Lora was reeling in a nice rainbow – the third one he had hooked in the pool.

By now, swarms of caddis were flying over the river, like snowflakes pushed by a strong wind.

"Grannoms," Rademacher announced.

The Grannom caddis, sometimes called the Shad Fly because it emerges when schools of American shad are spawning in the Delaware and other rivers, is a prolific insect that, like the Hendrickson, often provokes a trout feeding frenzy.

Many of the caddis were struggling and falling spent to the surface, but we looked in vain for the rings of rising trout.

Adrift once more, we saw an osprey swing across the valley, a fish clutched in its talons. Farther on, five turkey vultures flapped their cloak-like wings and alighted on the

Tim Wood of Otisco scans the surface for rising fish on the West Branch of the Delaware River near Hale Eddy.

beach beside a dead sucker.

Occasionally, Rademacher noted, a bald eagle patrols the same stretch of water and sky.

Shortly after noon we stopped our drift beside "Andre's Riffle," so-christened by Rademacher in honor of a fellow guide who counts the spot as his ace in the hole.

Lora checked his watch.

"We'd better eat before it's too dark to see our sandwiches," he said, laughing.

When we stuffed our paper bags back into the portable coolers, the eclipse was starting.

Lacking Mylar strips or index cards with pinholes in them, we dared not look directly at the sun, but stole quick glances over our shoulders at the appointed hour.

My enduring notion of an eclipse comes from that Bing

Crosby film classic, "An American Yankee in King Arthur's Court," in which our hero saves himself from burning at the stake by solemnly predicting that the sun will go out if he's not set free. The peasants whine and courtiers cower when Der Bingle makes good his threat.

The real eclipse could have used a touch of Hollywood. Its effect was soothing, as if a window shade had been drawn on a too-bright room. The sky was still blue and water still twinkled.

Frankly, the whole thing was a letdown.

Certainly the Hendricksons weren't impressed. At 2:02, more or less right on schedule, the first of the grayish-bodied insects fluttered off the river. Within minutes, hundreds were visible in every direction.

Downstream, where the riffles flattened out, feeding trout began to poke frothy white holes through the green surface of the river.

We clambered into the boat and, crouching like Marines in amphibious landing craft, glided toward the rising fish.

In the tail of the pool, a pod of six trout slashed at the emerging insects, but the water near them was too deep to wade, and the swirling currents made it impossible for Rademacher to hold the boat in casting position. Reluctantly, we made for the shore and looked for other trout. Several impressive risers fed in mid-river. When Lora and I waded as deep as we dared, they were still out of reach.

I was summoning the nerve to go one step deeper when a gust slung the fly around my neck and rain began to fall.

It seemed the eclipse was the least of the tricks Mother

Nature had in store for us.

During the next three hours, Hendricksons hatched sporadically, but swirling winds frequently made accurate casting impossible. The few trout that rose were on the far side of the river – no matter which side we chose to wade.

As we floated through the pool above the Buckingham boat ramp, the river issued a final taunt. A dozen dimples pockmarked the smooth water, as big trout sipped spent mayflies and caddis.

Instead of holding in one place and letting the food come to them, as trout typically do in fast currents, these calm-water fish wandered left, right or dead ahead at a whim.

It was like leading ducks with a shotgun, except the shooters were blindfolded. Lora and I lucked into one rise apiece, but most of the afternoon we managed to cast where the fish weren't.

As we unloaded our gear and cranked the boat back onto its trailer, four Pennsylvania fishermen got out of their car and waded into the river, hoping for an evening hatch.

But the trout had stopped rising, and the current rushing past the launch ram was as flat as a table top.

"Did you do any good?" Rademacher asked one of the anglers.

"It was a frustrating day," the fisherman admitted. "The water's too high and it was much too windy."

With a wink and a smile, he added one more excuse to the traditional post-fishing trip litany of blame.

"Plus, that eclipse really screwed things up," he said.

HOMESPUN ANGLERS
March 31, 2006

Since 1977, when they began keeping an angling diary, the Andrews family of Pompey has caught a grand total of 6,034 fish during their annual, week-long vacations on the Ogdensburg stretch of the St. Lawrence River.

They have stacks of photos to prove it, too – grip-and-grin shots of family members with lunker smallmouth bass, walleyes and northern pike against a riverine backdrop.

Remarkably, they hooked virtually all of those beauties on homemade spinners, tipped with worms.

"We couldn't afford to fish the way we do if we didn't make our own lures," said the oldest of four Andrews brothers, Tom, 53.

The family has been visiting the St. Lawrence in early August for about 40 years.

"We go then because it fits in with our farm-work schedule," Tom said.

He and brother Jerry, 49, who both live on the family farm; and John, 34, of Mattydale usually make the trip with their mother, Ramona.

Ramona's husband, Jim, has been unable to fish in recent years due to health problems. Their fourth son, Michael, 50, of Fabius; and his wife, Sue, take care of the farm when the other family members are away.

It didn't take many days on the river for the Andrews

to figure out that drifting over deep rocks was a very productive way to catch smallmouth bass.

"Mom started using spinners and worms that way, and she was catching more fish than we were," Tom said. "But you lose an awful lot of tackle when you're fishing on those rocks, so before long we started making our own spinners."

Over the years, the Andrews have filled and re-filled their tackle boxes with lures. They figure they've saved thousands of dollars along the way.

The family members got their lure-making education by reading books on the subject – Boyd Pfeiffer's "Tacklecraft" is a favorite – and by browsing through the back pages of Field & Stream magazine for the names of parts suppliers.

They purchase most of their lure components from Jann's Netcraft, a catalog merchant in Maumee, Ohio.

"They have everything you could possibly want," Ramona said.

Well, not quite.

For along with the spinner blades, beads, coils of wire and other parts from Netcraft, the Andrews incorporate plenty of what-nots acquired from garage sales and craft shops into their lures.

Ramona has fashioned quite a few successfully fish-takers from drop-style ear rings.

"The cheaper and gaudier, the better they are for lures," she said.

Nor should lure-makers overlook the beauty supply shelves of local drug stores and supermarkets.

Often, after he's fashioned a spinner in his $16 "Tackle

Tool" vise, Tom reaches for a bottle of nail polish.

"It makes a very serviceable paint," he said.

The family literally has a shoebox full of the stuff, in every conceivable color from hot pink to black to deep purple.

However, year-in, year-out, Tom's most reliable spinner is one with a plain gold-finish, willow leaf-shaped blade and red and yellow plastic beads on the wire shaft.

"I usually just add a size 1 or 1/0 hook to it," he said.

Ramona stocks up on willow leaf lures, too, although her tackle box also contains plenty of spinners made with the rounder Colorado and Indiana-shaped blades.

Her all-time favorite lure will never be used. It has a red, heart-shaped blade, inscribed with the words "We love you" in white nail polish.

"The boys gave me the new one for a Valentine's Day present," she said.

Making lures on cold winter nights when the wind is rattling the farmhouse windows always unlocks a vault of memories.

Sifting through the family pictures, Jerry came up with a photo of his first walleye.

"Twenty-four inches," he declared, after confirming the measurements in the family's spiral-bound logbook. It took one of those homemade spinners, of course.

John produced a recent snapshot of himself with a 5-pound channel catfish. During the battle with that bewhiskered lunker, he stripped the gears on his reel and wound up hauling in fishing line hand over hand. Later,

Tom repaired the old Zebco reel, using gears he located on the Internet.

"I didn't want to replace it because it was a graduation present and it meant a lot to me," John said.

Ramona's tackle box is also a treasured gift.

It was 1971. Tom, soon after graduating from the University of Buffalo, had been drafted and inducted into the Army.

Naturally, Ramona was very worried about her son.

Part way through basic training, Tom got a Christmas pass out of Ft. Dix. On Christmas eve, which also happens to be Ramona's birthday, he and his father went shopping and purchased the tackle box.

"She'd had her eye on that box all year, and it was the last one of its kind in the store," Tom said. "I don't know about Mom, but that was my best Christmas, ever."

JULY OFFERS FISHERMEN SOME NICE DISTRACTIONS
July 13, 2003

July may not be the likeliest time to catch a trout, yet surely is one of the more rewarding months of the year to be trout fishing.

One afternoon last week I hiked into a favorite stretch of water over an abandoned road and a barely discernable foot path.

Before I had even strung up my fly rod, I came across a wild rose bush, the last remnant of a house that burned to the ground nearly 20 years ago. The shocking pink flowers glowed like a beacon in an overgrown meadow.

Beside the narrow path were several fresh deer beds, including one oval of flattened grass no more than two feet in diameter. The white-speckled fawn that made the impression was still nursing at its mother's breast and tottering on wobbly legs.

When I broke out of the woods and heard the rushing water in the creek, a great blue heron as big as a pterodactyl flapped its wings and sailed around the bend.

The trout were shy, as they usually are on a hot summer day, but I managed to catch a few in the next couple of hours. None were of notable size, but each sparkled in a summer-best coat of many colors. Serenaded by songbirds, I never thought to look at my watch until I had fished all the way back to the bridge.

Along the road was a clump of day lilies, surrounded by garlands of sweet peas. It took a bush full of black raspberries to tear my eyes away from that pretty sight.

Climbing the hill toward the car, I found several glossy brown feathers, and scuffed-up leaves where that same turkey had rummaged for insects and sprouts of fresh greenery. Just beyond the bird's pantry was a pile of coyote scat, full of cottontail rabbit fur.

Any angler who can't find the time for distractions like these needs to take life a little easier.

THE BEST AND WORST OF TIMES FOR A TROUT ANGLER
August 17, 1993

I spent my last vacation traveling through time.

One leg of the journey took me into trout-fishing's past, where the view was uplifting and glorious.

The other fork in the road plunged toward a dark and gloomy future where I could see nothing but trouble.

The time machine slipped into reverse on the banks of Letort Spring Creek, just south of Carlisle, PA.

Crickets chirped in the sun-splashed meadows by the bridge at Bonnybrook Road. Another fisherman was fiddling with his tackle as I pulled into the parking area.

"Any luck?" I asked.

"Just starting," the stranger replied. "Thought I'd hike down to Fox's meadow for the afternoon."

I admitted I had made just one previous visit to the creek, and wasn't sure where to fish.

"Well, if you'd like a tour, you're welcome to tag along with me," the stranger said.

As easily as that I became friends with Mike "Always" Ready, a trout fanatic who flexes his fly rod on the Letort at least four or five times a week.

The Letort is a spring-fed stream famed for its population of wary, wild trout. Ten years ago, Ready took a 27 ½-inch brown from one of its crystalline pools. Yet the possibility of hooking another monster is only one reason he haunts the stream.

Angling history was written on the currents of the Letort, and the fisherman who stalks trout in the two-mile stretch between Bonnybrook Road and the Interstate 81 overpass wets his line in a living museum.

"I love to show people this place," Ready said.

The Letort was the laboratory for Vincent Marinaro, the late resident of Carlisle who authored "A Modern Dry-Fly Code," one of the classics in fly-fishing literature. The 1950 volume codified methods of catching trout on flies that imitate terrestrial insects, among other breakthroughs.

Ready pointed out the wooden bench where Marinaro sat while he studied rising fish in his favorite pool, and the stone monument that the author's admirers placed beside the Letort in his memory.

Charlie Fox, who still lives in a farmhouse overlooking the creek, was another pioneer. The author of several popular fishing books, Fox is revered by Carlisle anglers for the physical labor he poured into local waters. With the assistance of Marinaro and others, he spread 20 tons of fine gravel across silty sections of the Letort, then laid protective horseshoes of limestone rock to create spawning channels for his beloved trout.

"If you come back in November, you'll see some huge browns spawning right there," Ready said.

I failed to hook a single fish after parting company with Ready that afternoon, yet I felt refreshed and enriched by the time spent with brother anglers, living and dead.

A visit to Factory Brook, in contrast, carved a hole in

my heart.

Cliff Creech, the regional natural resources manager for the Department of Environmental Conservation, had shown me a trick or two that day, and we were thoroughly enjoying ourselves until we came upon a pair of boys fishing at the Route 41 bridge in the village of Homer.

"Catching any?" Creech asked them.

The chubby blond with the Huckleberry Finn freckles pointed to a stringer hanging from the wire gabions along the brook channel. It was laden with trout – five browns and three brookies.

We were about to express our admiration when Huck suddenly jerked his rod. Missing the target, he hurled the treble hook into the water and yanked again.

The boys were snagging. All of their fish had been stabbed in their bellies or fins by bare, unbaited hooks.

"Don't do that," Creech said, in a half-warning, half-pleading tone.

"Why not?" Huck replied. "It's fun."

"It's illegal," I shot back. "It's not fair to the fish or to other fishermen who play by the rules."

At that point, Huck's pal joined the conversation.

"But mister," he said. "I'm just a kid. I don't know any better."

He snickered at his little joke and resumed casting and yanking.

We warned the boys, who looked to be 11 or 12 years old, that we would call the local conservation officer if they persisted. They hooted at that one.

Exasperated, we left to look for a public telephone.

When we drove back across the bridge a few minutes later the young poachers had vanished.

"At least we scared them a little," I said.

In truth, I was the one who was scared. Scared of the damage these boys and others like them would wreak on Factory Brook and other streams before they grew up. Scared of the lessons they would pass on to their own children.

And scared, most of all, that trout-fishing's future will not be worthy of its past.

FRIEND'S SPIRIT FLIES IN FACE OF DEATH
July 19, 1994

Ten years ago, when we gathered beside the bend on Nine Mile Creek to say good-bye to Dan Skinner, sulfur mayflies were hatching, and the stream's surface was dimpled by the rings of rising trout.

I could almost picture the redhead standing there, sunburned and sweating, rod in hand, poised for a strike.

Then a car door slammed shut and Dan's girlfriend, Ginny, walked up the gravel beach, clutching a ceramic urn to her waist.

Thirty of us, relatives, neighbors, schoolmates and co-workers of Dan's, fell silent.

Ginny said Dan had requested that his ashes be spread upon the waters of Nine Mile Creek because he had spent so many happy hours here. He chose this pool, she said with a smile, not because the fishing was especially good but because there was plenty of parking nearby. Then she invited several of us to say a few words about Dan. The years whirled by while I waited my turn.

Dan and I had been best friends since elementary school. I first saw him with his brother, Ed, being towed down our snow-covered street on a sled by a big, speckled English pointer. Before we were 12 years old we had the bad habit of walking into each other's houses at any time of day without knocking. We played football under the

Dan Skinner fished and hunted as hard as he could until cancer finally caught up with him.

street lights on the Methodist Church lawn, fished for rock bass in Marcellus Park and bought candy bars – six for a quarter – at Hickman's Corner Store. As teenagers, we hunted pheasants, rabbits, woodcock and grouse.

Though inseparable, we often went in opposite directions. I was inclined to conformity, and Dan was a proud square peg. We studied the Baltimore Catechism side by side in release-time religion classes, but the Catholicism I embraced Dan shed like a scratchy wool coat. Sometimes, fortified in his faithlessness by Guinness Stout, he would rail against organized religion, to my discomfort and the consternation of his devout and devoted mother.

Though blessed with a brilliant mind, Dan chafed at the very notion of studiousness, and if a school subject did not catch his fancy, he would coast to a C instead of climbing toward the A that was always within his reach. Teachers bemoaned Dan's unfulfilled potential. He surprised most of them by winning a Regents scholarship, then vindicated their initial judgement by dropping out of college after his freshman year. Later, he bounced from job to job, never quite finding a perfect fit.

Through his own ups and downs, Dan kept his friends laughing.

At school dances, he did the Charleston to rock and roll rhythms. He could recite the entire Gettysburg Address in spoonerisms, and perfected a goofy, cocked-hat impression of Truman Capote.

The jokes fell flat the night he told me about his cancer.

At the time, both of us were in our late '20s, married, and slowly being tugged apart as childhood friends